Library of
Davidson College

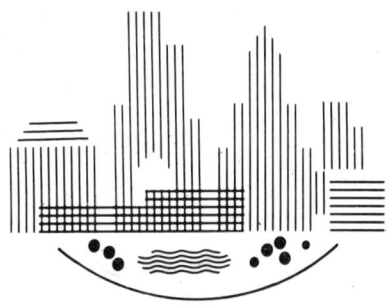

THE RISE OF URBAN AMERICA

ADVISORY EDITOR
Richard C. Wade
PROFESSOR OF AMERICAN HISTORY
UNIVERSITY OF CHICAGO

THE TWENTIETH CENTURY CITY

Josiah Strong

ARNO PRESS
&
The New York Times
NEW YORK • 1970

Reprint Edition 1970 by Arno Press Inc.

Reprinted from a copy in The University of Illinois Library

LC# 77-112575
ISBN 0-405-02477-0

THE RISE OF URBAN AMERICA
ISBN for complete set 0-405-02430-4

Manufactured in the United States of America

The Twentieth Century City

BY

REV. JOSIAH STRONG, D.D.

General Secretary of the Evangelical Alliance for the United States
Author of "Our Country" and "The New Era"

FIFTEENTH THOUSAND

"He who makes the city makes the world"
—*Drummond*

"In proportion as the structure of a government gives force to public opinion, it is essential that public opinion should be enlightened"
—*Washington*

NEW YORK
THE BAKER AND TAYLOR CO.
33–37 EAST SEVENTEENTH STREET
UNION SQUARE, NORTH

COPYRIGHT, 1898, BY
THE BAKER & TAYLOR CO.

PREFACE

THIS book attempts both a diagnosis and a prescription. It undertakes to show the essential character of modern civilization, its weakness and its peril: and suggests a treatment which is obviously practicable. The effectiveness of the proposed treatment can be determined only by actual test, but the strong confidence in its value which has been expressed with singular unanimity, by many of the most eminent statesmen, educators, editors, and clergymen of the land, certainly calls for a faithful application of the proposed remedy.

Preface

Somewhat over half of the material of the book appeared recently as a series of articles in *The Christian Advocate.* The generous reception accorded to them by the public has called for their expansion and for their publication in a more permanent form.

J. S.

NEW YORK, March, 1898.

CONTENTS

CHAPTER I

THE MATERIALISM OF MODERN CIVILIZATION.
Page 11

The necessity of a parity of growth between the physical, mental, and moral. The order of development. Spain and England. The process of degeneration.

The material side of modern civilization. Increase in our knowledge of matter. Resulting scepticism. Increase of power. Steam-power of United States, Great Britain, Germany, and France. Increase of wealth. Mr. Gladstone's estimate.

Materialism of American civilization. Causes. Development during nineteenth century: commonwealths; cities; population; agriculture; railways; telegraph lines; working-power of the nation; wealth. Effect of wealth.

The city the best exponent of modern materialistic civilization. New York. Cities of the Old World.

CHAPTER II

A NATION OF CITIES......................*Page* 33

Phenomenal growth of modern city due to redistribution of population. Three causes: 1. Application of machinery to agriculture. Necessary limit to demand for farm products. Effect of excessive supply. Effect of scientific methods. Agriculture to be confined to a decreasing proportion of population.

2. Substitution of mechanical power for muscular, and its application to manufactures. Application of machinery to agriculture and to manufactures produced opposite results; cause. Dr. Engel's law. Effect on growth of city.

v

Contents

3. The railway. Easy transportation of food. These causes permanent. Tendency of population toward city permanent.
Folly of fighting economic laws. The cry "Back to the soil" fallacious. The age of homespun. Two effects of the application of mechanical power to manufactures; the organization of industry; the increase of products. Elevation of the standard of living compels the farmer to produce for the market. Population transferred from city to farm would drive population from farm to city.
Scientific farming, instead of retarding migration from country to city would quicken it. Nevertheless we must make our farming scientific or lose our European markets for agricultural products. Must face the inevitable growth of the city.

CHAPTER III

THE MATERIALISTIC CITY A MENACE TO ITSELF.

Page 55

What constitutes a materialistic city. The demand which the twentieth century city will make on a higher intelligence. The problems of wealth. Its disproportionate increase in the city. Sanitary problems. Death-rate. Problems of government increase with population. The city in the experimental stage. Ignorance in control of our largest cities. Illustrated.
Increasing demands made on moral character by the city. Division of labor, and increasing dependence. Mrs. Browning quoted. Interdependence of allied industries. Men must become more dependable, must better appreciate mutual obligations. Stronger temptations.
Moral growth has not kept pace with the material. Chicago. Professor Bryce quoted. The spirit of lawlessness. Crime in Philadelphia and Pittsburg as compared with rural counties. Prospect. Mr. Lecky quoted. The roots of moral life growing weaker; the home; the church. James Freeman Clarke quoted.
Materialism and the city slum. Professor Huxley on

Contents

the East End of London. Elements of social dynamite. Problem complicated by heterogeneous character of American cities.

CHAPTER IV

THE MATERIALISTIC CITY A MENACE TO STATE AND NATION............................*Page* 81

De Tocqueville quoted on local self-government and on the city's menace to liberty. Professor Bryce and Professor Giddings quoted. The surrender of fundamental principles. The way our cities lost autonomy. The centralization of power and its significance. Forcing the intelligence and character of the city to unite in the wise choice of a mayor by the magnitude of the stake; illustrated by first election of Greater New York. Failure of democracy in large cities.

Gravity of the fact that the city will soon dominate the nation. The situation in 1920. The Goddess of Liberty leaning on a bayonet.

Who is to control the city when the city controls state and nation? Saloon-keepers. Ecclesiastics. Foreigners by birth or parentage. The time foretold by Wendell Phillips drawing near. Our probation in which to prepare for it none too long.

CHAPTER V

REMEDIES—THE NEW PATRIOTISM........*Page* 103

Sacrificing the public good to private gain. The "good citizen" the accomplice of the bad. Kossuth quoted. The lack of civic patriotism.

Two fundamental principles in the structure of our government. The one endangered at time of the civil war; the other endangered now by bossism. Military patriotism defended the former; civic patriotism must defend the latter.

The new patriotism must be courageous; tireless; stronger than partisanship. The boss the product of the political situation. Necessity of education. "The Heroic Age;" Richard Watson Gilder quoted.

Contents

CHAPTER VI

REMEDIES — TWENTIETH CENTURY CHRISTIANITY.
Page 116

New social problems and the social teachings of Jesus.

A dawning social self-consciousness is bringing a social conscience, a new social spirit, and a new social ideal.

The social conscience emphasizes duties, and is the promise of many reforms. The new social spirit emphasizes fraternity and promises co-operation. The new social ideal awakes the hope of a perfected civilization.

The new social ideal, when Christianized, becomes the Kingdom of God fully come in the earth. The new social spirit when Christianized becomes not a fraternity of convenience but of brotherly love. The new social conscience can be adequately instructed only by the social teachings of Jesus.

How can the social organism be perfected? Only by obeying two laws fundamental to every living organism: the law of service; the law of sacrifice. These laws very imperfectly obeyed, hence social disease.

Jesus taught three social laws, which are fundamental to Christianity: the law of service; the law of sacrifice; the law of love. The latter vitalizes the other two. Society, therefore, will be perfected when love is accepted as its law.

CHAPTER VII

REMEDIES — TWENTIETH CENTURY CHURCHES.
Page 131

As the teachings of Jesus, applied to social problems, would solve them, it is the duty of the churches to make the application. Dr. C. H. Payne quoted. The churches must save society, or themselves perish. Bishop Potter quoted.

Duty of the churches to educate the social conscience.

Contents

Fallacious distinction between the sacred and the "secular." Churches must instruct as to all manward obligations. Bishop Huntington quoted.
The new social spirit is fraternal. Love must be inculcated by the churches as the fundamental law of normal social life. Fallacious substitutes. Churches have not believed in the practicability of Christ's teachings.
The Kingdom of God fully come in the earth is the true social ideal. Christ's social ideal lays upon the churches a social mission. The "gospel of the Kingdom" a social gospel. Mission of the churches to society no less sacred than that to the individual. Theoretical objection answered by actual facts.
Important distinction between the Church and the Kingdom. Churches which belie Christ. Commercialism in religion.

CHAPTER VIII

REMEDIES—PRACTICAL SUGGESTIONS......*Page* 153

The extraordinary situation which confronts us requires extraordinary provision. The education of public opinion and of the popular conscience the generic reform. The three classes into which every new reform divides society. How to reach the indifferent, the great problem. Truth must be taken to them, utilizing the young people's societies. Character of the literature to be scattered.
We have popularized bad literature. The sensational and criminal press. French fiction. Obscene literature. Cowper quoted. Must fight the bad press with the good press.
Necessity of applying an enlightened public opinion and a quickened conscience to legislation. No existing medium through which the application can be made. The proposed medium. Amounts to the *referendum*. Bryce quoted. Proposed method will enable the churches to accomplish the reforms demanded by applied Christianity. Urgency of the need. The first city and the last.

The Twentieth Century City

I

The Materialism of Modern Civilization

As we stand on the threshold of a new century, it is natural to look into the past and to desire to look into the future. If we glance over our shoulder at some of the most significant changes of the past hundred years and note their tendencies, we shall find that looking backward will enable us to look forward, because tendencies are prophetic.

The nineteenth century has given birth to many marvels, but beyond question its greatest and most characteristic wonder has been the unprecedented and disproportionate development of material civilization.

I say disproportionate, because in the development of civilization, as in that of the individual, there should be, between the physical, mental, and moral, a parity of growth. If the child grows in body but not in mind, he becomes an idiot. If he develops physically and mentally, but not morally, he becomes a criminal. History has taught no lesson with more emphasis than this, that ignorant or unscrupulous power is dangerous. As the child grows in stature, there should be a growing moral sense and an increasing intelligence to restrain and direct his increasing strength, otherwise he will inflict injury both upon himself and others; and society, because it is composed of individuals, should show the same harmony of development.

There cannot be a high intellectual

and spiritual growth without an adequate physical basis. Man is the most perfect animal in the world. It was the highest physical organism which received the double crown of intellectual and spiritual life. In human experience, the higher is conditioned by the lower, as the superstructure is limited by the foundation. But it is quite possible to develop the lower life at the expense of the higher. The splendid physique of the prize-fighter does not imply a corresponding intellectual and spiritual development, but quite the contrary. As an animal, he is admirable; as a man, he is monstrous.

Some plant-life, when the soil is very rich, runs to root and top, and produces little or no bloom and fruit. We cannot have the fruit without top and root, but there is a misdirection of plant-energy when their growth is at the expense of fruit.

The Twentieth Century City

It is a vital question whether the materialism of the nineteenth century is to blossom into something higher in the twentieth, or whether our marvellous material civilization will prove to be at the expense of intellectual and spiritual growth.

The order of development is the lower first; "time's noblest offspring is the last." The apostle says: "First, that which is natural, then that which is spiritual." Child-life is, first, animal; later, intelligence dawns, and, last of all, the moral and spiritual life. History would seem to show that this is the natural order in the progress of civilization; that great intellectual expansion and spiritual quickening are usually preceded by a material advance; and if such material growth is not followed by an intellectual and moral advance, degeneration takes place.

The great Reformation and the lit-

Modern Materialism

erary splendor of the sixteenth century followed a period of wonderful physical activity. There were voyages, travels, inventions, discoveries, which resulted in a great extension of commerce and increase of wealth. The gold of the New World was poured into the lap of Spain; but Spain failed to make a corresponding development of intellectual and spiritual life, and her material glory soon faded. England, on the other hand, made intellectual and moral progress no less remarkable than her physical growth. Increasing wealth, therefore, did not corrupt and weaken her. Her higher life was able to control the lower, and thus prepared the way for a still wider material expansion.

Without an adequate moral development to control the physical and utilize it for ends above itself, the material becomes sensuous, then sensual; and sensuality means decay and death.

The Twentieth Century City

This process of degeneration was illustrated by Greece and Rome, and by all of the ancient civilizations of the East. They perished for lack of parity of growth. Their material development, which was once their glory, became at length their weakness and destruction.

Glance now at the progress of modern civilization on its material side. There has been a wonderful increase in our knowledge of matter. Indeed, the physical sciences have most of them been created during this century. The microscope has given to us many a Columbus, each of whom has discovered, not a new continent, but a new world, of which we had never dreamed. The scientific mind and method have made opulent increase in our knowledge of matter and its laws, which is well; but there has been no corresponding increase in our knowledge of spirit and its laws.

Modern Materialism

We have fixed our close and prolonged attention on things, and things are below us. Only spirit is above us; only spirit can furnish us lofty ideals which beckon us above ourselves.

The exclusive study of matter has to many minds made spirit seem unreal and cast a doubt on immortality, thus reviving the "philosophy of dirt," which is as old as Democritus and Lucretius; while the many who care nothing for speculative thought have accepted a practical materialism, which deems real and worth while only that which can be weighed and measured, bought and sold. Thus, scepticism has become wide-spread; and as the decay of faith is naturally followed by a lusty growth of credulity, strange and heathenish beliefs have appeared, which easily disciple men and women who have "outgrown" the Christian religion. When men are so incred-

The Twentieth Century City

ulous as to reject the reasonable, they are always sufficiently credulous to accept the unreasonable.

The growth of the physical sciences has resulted in a mastery of natural laws and forces, which has enormously lengthened the leverage of our power. In the United States, Great Britain, Germany, and France there is steam-power at work equal to the strength of 551,600,000 able-bodied men. Here we have in these four countries, on the average, two and four-fifths mechanical slaves to every man, woman, and child, or fourteen to every family of five; and the organization of this power makes it vastly more than seven times as productive as the isolated power of the parents to whom the family of five looks for support. In the above estimate no account is made of horse, water, wind, or electrical power, which would aggregate nearly as much more. Nor is

Modern Materialism

the almost endless amount of machinery included through which steam-power is applied, and which is ten, twenty, and, in some cases, even a hundred times as effective as power applied by hand.

It is not strange that so immense an increase of power should be accompanied by a like increase of wealth, to the production of which it has been applied. For a comparison of the world's wealth in the nineteenth and preceding centuries, we of course have no exact data, but may refer to Mr. Gladstone's well-known estimate that all the wealth which could be handed down to posterity, produced during the first eighteen hundred years of the Christian era, was equalled by the production of the first fifty years of the nineteenth century, and that as much more was produced during the next twenty years. If this is a reasonable estimate, as it would

The Twentieth Century City

seem to be, it is safe to say, that for the enrichment of the world there has been more than three times as much wealth produced during this one century as during the eighteen centuries preceding.

The materialism of modern civilization is better illustrated perhaps in this country than anywhere else in Christendom. Not that we are more worldly and less Christian than other peoples, but peculiar conditions in the United States have made the pursuit of material good more eager, more intense and absorbing, here than anywhere else in the world.

At the beginning of the century our national territory was less than one-fourth of its present area, and only a small proportion of that was settled. Here was an opportunity for expansion without a parallel, and the use made of it is without a precedent. In bringing this continental wilder-

Modern Materialism

ness under the yoke of civilization, we have during this century organized twenty-nine great commonwealths, twenty-four of which are each larger than all England, and the average area of the twenty-nine is greater than that of England, Wales, and Denmark in one. Each of these empires has been provided with the homes, the schools, the colleges, the churches, the press, the agriculture, the manufactures, the commerce, the government, the laws, the courts, and the established usages of civilized society.

During ninety years of this century our population increased fifty-seven and a half millions, or nearly twelve hundred per cent.

We have since 1800 built over four hundred cities, among which are some of the great cities of the world, and all of the older and larger ones have been rebuilt several times.

The Twentieth Century City

Up to 1890 we had brought under cultivation 4,564,000 farms, comprising upward of 623,000,000 acres. From 1850 to 1890 the area of our farms was increased by 245,000,000 acres, an average of 16,000 acres every day. The new farms occupied and improved during these forty years are greater in area than the German Empire, England, Scotland, Ireland, Holland, Denmark, Belgium, and Switzerland, taken collectively.

Up to 1895 we had built 232,755 miles of railway, the construction and equipment of which cost $9,693,141,-000. In 1830 we had twenty-three miles of railway. Averaging the construction for the sixty-five years following, we built every year enough to cross the continent—3,000 miles from ocean to ocean—at the average annual cost of $149,000,000. During the last twenty years of this period we expended on new lines a million dollars a day.

Modern Materialism

The English statistician, Mr. Mulhall, wrote, in 1895; "The merchandise transported by rail in the United States is shown by official returns to be double the amount of land-carriage (at least by railway) of all the other nations of the earth collectively." What a comment on our industrial and commercial activity, that the 70,000,000 people of the United States transport by rail twice as much merchandise as the remaining 1,400,000,000 of mankind! In 1895 we had 802,000 miles of telegraph wire—enough to encircle the earth 32 times, or to cross the continent 267 times.

The energy or working-power of the nation, including hand, horse, and steam power, was equal, in 1895, to 129,306,000,000 foot-tons daily; that is, it was equal to lifting that number of tons one foot every day. Our working-power is more than twice as great as that of Great Britain, and is

The Twentieth Century City

nearly equal to that of Great Britain, Germany, and France combined.

With this power directed chiefly to the creation of wealth, it is not strange that we are growing rich more rapidly than any other people. Our wealth in 1820 was less than two thousand million dollars. In twenty years it had doubled, and in forty years it had increased eightfold. During the thirty years following, from 1860 to 1890, we created and accumulated forty-nine thousand million dollars— a thousand million dollars more than the entire wealth of Great Britain; and, nothwithstanding the great increase of population, our wealth *per caput* doubled during this interval.

The wealth of the Old World is the accumulation of many centuries, but ninety-four per cent. of ours has been created and accumulated since 1840; and we are now increasing it at the rate of $7,000,000 a day.

Modern Materialism

Surely "these American days are more marvellous than the 'Arabian Nights.'"

This vast wealth represents all material things. Since the advent of machinery the accessories of life have been multiplied beyond all inventory. Things, things, an endless variety of things! What is their effect on us? Do they minister to us simply, or do they enable us to minister more largely and effectively to others? If they end in us, affording new sensations to appetite, gratifying tastes only to re-refine them beyond gratification, economizing time only to invite idleness, and multiplying wants without enlarging life, then do they sensualize and corrupt us; and the more the accessories of life are multiplied, the more useless does life become and the sooner is it rendered a burden to itself.

If, on the other hand, the numberless appliances of civilization help us

The Twentieth Century City

to minister more largely and effectively to the world's needs; if facilities of travel and communication, improved tools and perfected processes, enable us to do two years' work in one, or to influence for good a thousand instead of a hundred, then is life en-enlarged, enriched, and ennobled, gold is transmuted into character, the material is spiritualized, and the kingdom of heaven comes apace.

During this century each generation in the United States has been able to hand down to the succeeding, four or five times as much wealth as it received from the preceding. The inheritance of great riches usually leads to one of three results, viz.: self-indulgence and enervation—a life of wallowing in wealth; or avarice and hardness—a life of mere money-getting and keeping; or a self-mastery which saves from both of these pitfalls—a life which recognizes the

Modern Materialism

power in wealth as a sacred trust, to be used for the benefit of mankind—a character which, with the strength of a noble purpose, unites the beauty of the best culture. But it is to be feared that our increasing wealth is producing fewer philanthropists than sensualists and misers. Is it not the prevailing tendency of modern material civilization to stimulate luxury and to inflame avarice? And in view of the fact that luxury is historically debilitating and demoralizing, are we not forced to conclude that our disproportionate material progress has become perilous?

We must not forget that during this century intellectual and moral progress has been real and great. There has been a wide diffusion of knowledge, and the average man is far more intelligent than his grandfather was. There has been an elevation of moral standards, though in

The Twentieth Century City

some important particulars they are now being lowered. The world is more Christian than it was a hundred years ago, and conscience is better educated. But intellectual and moral progress has by no means kept pace with material development.

There are many intelligent men who think the world is growing worse. I cannot agree with them. I believe that, on the whole, the sun sets on a better world every night. But the fact that many hold the contrary, shows that our moral progress is not indisputable, while our material progress is. No one questions the reality or the magnitude of the latter. The increase of material wealth is simply prodigious. There has been no corresponding increase in our wealth of literature and of noble ideals; no such massing of moral and spiritual treasure. It is not intemperate to say that there has been more material progress

Modern Materialism

during the nineteenth century than during the entire preceding history of the race. No one would think of making a similar statement concerning the intellectual and moral advancement of mankind; nor would anyone venture the assertion that we in America have surpassed European peoples in moral and intellectual growth as we have in material development.

If, now, it is true of modern civilization that materialism is its supreme peril, pre-eminently true is it of American civilization; and if material growth finds its comparative in the New World, the modern city furnishes its superlative. The modern city is at the same time the most characteristic product and the best exponent of modern civilization. Its growth in population and wealth, during this century, has been phenomenal, and quite out of proportion to that of the country at large.

The Twentieth Century City

Let New York illustrate the city's increasing rate of growth in recent times. Founded in 1614, it took New York 175 years to gain 33,000 inhabitants. During the next period of 50 years it gained 280,000; during the next 30 years it gained 630,000; and during the next 21 years, which period closed in 1890, it gained 859,000. The gain during the last short period was 26 times as large as during the first long period, and the rate of gain 208 times as great.

A hundred years ago the United States had only six cities of 8,000 inhabitants or more; in 1880, 286; and in 1890, 443. A hundred years ago three per cent. of our population was urban; now about thirty per cent.

Some have supposed that this remarkable movement of population from country to city was due to the exceptional conditions of a new civilization, which would pass with time.

Modern Materialism

But it is not peculiar to new civilizations. London is probably two thousand years old, and yet four-fifths of its growth have been added during this century. For sixty years Berlin has grown far more rapidly than New York. Paris is more than four times as large as it was in 1800. Rome has doubled since 1870. St. Petersburg has increased nearly threefold in seventy-five years. Odessa is a thousand years old, but nineteen-twentieths of its population have been added during this century. Calcutta has increased four hundred and sixty per cent. in seventy years. In Europe, Asia, and Africa we find this movement of population from country to city. It is a world-phenomenon.

Some have imagined that it would prove temporary; that this flowing tide would soon ebb. But its causes, which will be discussed in the next chapter, are permanent, and indicate

The Twentieth Century City

that this movement will be permanent. The sudden expansion of the city marks a profound change in civilization, the results of which will grow more and more obvious; and nowhere probably will this change be so significant as in our own country, where the twentieth century city will be decisive of national destiny.

II

A Nation of Cities

IN earlier ages population gathered chiefly in cities, but for reasons which were temporary. Men sought the protection from marauders which was afforded by the walled towns. They went to their fields in the morning, and returned at night. But with the establishment of social order the men who tilled the soil began to live on it. The growth of the modern city is due to causes which are permanent.

Foreign immigration has stimulated the growth of cities in the United States, but of course cannot account for the scarcely less surprising growth of European cities. The phenomenal growth of the modern city is due to a redistribution of population. From

The Twentieth Century City

1880 to 1890 urban population in the United States increased sixty-one per cent., while rural population increased only fourteen per cent., and 10,063 townships—thirty-nine per cent. of the whole number in 1880—actually lost population. Thus, Chicago more than doubled, while seven hundred and ninety-two townships in Illinois were depleted.

This redistribution of population is due to three principal causes:

1. The application of machinery to agriculture. A special agent of the Government reports that four men with improved agricultural implements now do the work formerly done by fourteen. Inasmuch as the world cannot eat three or four times as much food simply to oblige the farmers, a large proportion of them are compelled to abandon agriculture, and are forced into the towns and cities. Simply bearing in mind that the world's capacity

A Nation of Cities

to consume food is limited, will throw not a little light on economic conditions, both present and future. It means that only a limited number of persons can get a living by agriculture, and that when the supply of food has reached the limit of demand, agriculture can increase only as population increases.

To increase the food-supply beyond this limit serves only to decrease the farmers' income. In 1888 American farmers cultivated 25,000,000 acres more than in 1880, and their total cereal product was 491,000,000 bushels greater; but they received for it $41,000,000 less than for the smaller crops of 1880.

The fact that for a number of years the world's agriculture has been generally depressed would seem to show that supply reached the limit of the world's demand some time since. It is true there is want, even to starvation, but that is for lack of distribution, not for lack of adequate production. Quite as many people would go hungry in Chicago, if there were twice as many bushels of grain stored in the city's elevators.

Even the increase of population will not, for many years to come, require any increase in the number of farmers, because improved methods ought to increase the product as rapidly as increasing demand will require, until we have reached a much higher standard of agriculture. If scientific methods were generally adopted, we might undoubtedly double our product without any increase in acreage or in the number of farm-laborers.

It is true that as wealth increases a people will spend more on their table, though they do not eat more ; and the consumption of more expensive food offers increased opportunities to agriculture, but, as we shall see later, ex-

A Nation of Cities

penditure for subsistence does not keep even pace with increasing income.

After taking all the facts into consideration, we are forced to the conclusion that progress in agriculture will limit it to an ever-decreasing proportion of the population, which, of course, means that an ever-increasing proportion will live in cities.

2. The second great cause of the modern city's growth was the substitution of mechanical power for muscular, and its application to manufactures.

The world's work was formerly done by muscles; and the word "manufacturer" originally meant one who makes by hand. The change which has taken place in the meaning of the word suggests the industrial revolution which has been caused by the transition from muscular to mechanical power.

The Twentieth Century City

When the world's power was muscular, industry was for the most part individual, and naturally so. When power became mechanical and stationary, workmen gathered around it, and industry naturally became organized. Manufactures, therefore, meant the concentration of population.

The springing up of factories in the city to produce agricultural implements and a thousand other things, created a demand for labor, and attracted to the city the laborers who were being driven from the farms. It should be observed, in this connection, that the application of machinery to agriculture and to manufactures has in one particular produced opposite results. While it has reduced the proportion engaged in the former, it has increased the proportion engaged in the latter. In 1840, 21.79 per cent. of our population were engaged in agriculture; in 1870 the proportion

A Nation of Cities

had fallen to 15.43 per cent.; in 1880 it was 15.38 per cent., and in 1890 only 13.68 per cent. On the other hand, 4.12 per cent. of the population were employed in manufactures in 1850; 5.32 per cent. in 1870, and 7.52 per cent. in 1890. By the close of the century the proportion engaged in manufactures will be twice as large as it was fifty years before.

These opposite effects of machinery upon the two industries are of the greatest importance, since they are due to a cause which will continue operative, and will, therefore, shift these proportions more and more, perpetuating the movement of population from country to city. This cause is the fact that there is a natural limit to the world's capacity to consume food, while there is no such limit to its capacity to use the products of the mechanical arts. A family eats no more now than a family of the same

The Twentieth Century City

size at the beginning of the century (though they eat better food), but their home is supplied with ten times as many manufactured articles, the number and cost of which may be indefinitely increased. If the world were a hundred times as rich as it is, it could not eat a hundred times as much, nor could it make its food cost a hundredfold more ; but it could easily spend a hundred times as much on public buildings and palaces, parks, and private grounds, equipage and furniture, books and art, dress and ornament. For all these, purse and taste set the only limit of expenditure. The world's agriculture must relatively decrease while its manufactures increase. From 1870 to 1880 the former increased only 8.58 per cent., while the latter increased 18.60 per cent. Agriculture fell somewhat behind the estimated increase of the world's population, while manufact-

A Nation of Cities

ures increased nearly twice as rapidly.

This harmonizes perfectly with what is known as Engel's economic law. Dr. Engel, formerly head of the Prussian Statistical Bureau, tells us that the percentage of outlay for subsistence grows smaller as the income grows larger, and that the percentage of outlay for sundries becomes greater as income increases.

From all this it follows that, as the world grows richer, which the civilized part of it is doing very fast, an ever-increasing proportion of its population must get their livelihood by means of the mechanical and of the fine arts, while an ever-decreasing proportion will subsist by agriculture —from which the disproportionate growth of the city follows as a natural inference.

3. The third great cause of the growth of the modern city is the rail-

The Twentieth Century City

way, which makes it easy to transport population from country to city, and, which is much more important, easy to transport food, thus making it possible to feed any number of millions massed at one point. Prior to railway civilization, local famines were not infrequent; now they are become practically impossible, removing a former check to the growth of great cities.

It should be observed that all these causes are permanent; the tendency which springs from them will, therefore, be permanent. Beyond a peradventure, an ever-increasing proportion of the world's population must live in cities. It will not be long before urban population will largely preponderate over rural in the United States, and in due time we shall be a nation of cities.

This tremendous migration of millions from country to city, which

A Nation of Cities

marks a new civilization, is creating new social problems, and, as we shall see later, will soon create most serious political problems. Many are loath to see that the growth of the city is inevitable, and are suggesting various ways in which to relieve its congestion.

It is thought that if life on the farm can be rendered less distasteful, the young people, who are now eager to go to the city, may be persuaded to remain. It is true the city is more attractive; human intercourse, multiplied conveniences, greater religious privileges, superior educational advantages, amusements, excitements, an endless variety of happenings — all these appeal strongly to preference, and have their influence; but these causes are subordinate. Even if these attractions could be made to preponderate in favor of the country, that would not materially retard the movement cityward. The decisive causes are economic, and they are absolutely compulsory; they do not consult preferences but create necessities.

Some philanthropists think that the congestion of the city might be relieved and the miseries of the slums alleviated by removing families to unoccupied lands; and many are under the impression that if the multitude could be got back to the soil, our most perplexing problems would be solved. But all such fail to appreciate the profound significance of the transition during this century, from muscular to mechanical power—the most important change which has ever taken place in the history of the world; one which has already wrought an industrial revolution, and is rapidly creating a new civilization. It has separated, as by an impassable gulf, the simple, homespun, individualistic life of the world's past, from the complex,

A Nation of Cities

closely associated life of the present and of the future.

In the age of homespun, which, for most of our population, reached nearly to the middle of this century, the typical farmer had little money, and little need of it. The industry and ingenuity of himself and of his good wife supplied nearly all the wants of their household. Together they could do in a rude way the work which now represents ten or a dozen trades. They could have reared a family in comparative comfort, if they had been cast away on Robinson Crusoe's island. They were practically independent of the whole world.

All this has been radically changed by the substitution of mechanical for muscular power, which has worked two most important results : first, the organization of industry; and second, a vast increase of products.

The organization of industry, of

course necessitated the division of labor, by which each of the twenty men, who operate the score of machines which now do the work of a single trade, becomes dependent on the other nineteen. In like manner, the great industries have become allied, each to all the others, constituting together an endless chain of interdependence. Thus have sprung up absolutely new industrial conditions, which are producing equally new social conditions.

Mechanical power, which admits of indefinite increase, together with the organization of industry, which greatly economizes power, has enormously increased production. An excellent statistician estimated a few years since that if the goods made in one year by the 3,000,000 factory-workers in the United States at that time had been made by hand, their production would have required the labor of 150,-

A Nation of Cities

000,000 persons; that is, the machine-method may be considered, on the average, about fifty times as productive as the old hand-method.

The immense increase of supply greatly stimulated demand and resulted in a remarkable elevation of the standard of living. With the rise of that standard, what at first were regarded as luxuries came to be considered conveniences or comforts, and were at length deemed necessities. There are those still living who remember when friction-matches were a luxury.

The hand-labor of the farmer and his wife, however diversified, soon proved unequal to the multiplying wants of a rising standard of living. They could supply themselves only by purchase, for which money was necessary. The farmer must therefore produce for the market. Thus, agriculture became a part of *organized* industry; and, like manufactures, came

The Twentieth Century City

under the law of supply and demand ; with this important difference, already pointed out, that there is a natural and necessary limit to the world's ability to consume food, while its consumption of manufactured articles is determined by purse and taste—a wholly artificial limit, which is constantly being widened.

This natural limit to the world's demand for food, though perfectly obvious when mentioned, necessitates conclusions which are by no means self-evident. It shows that all efforts to relieve the congestion of the city by removing population to unoccupied lands, must needs be futile. If a hundred thousand families could be transferred from city slums to the country, and so trained as to become successful farmers, which is more than doubtful, it would not in the slightest degree mitigate poverty or relieve the pressure of population upon the city.

A Nation of Cities

These hundred thousand farmers could succeed only by getting the market; and as the world would eat no more simply to accommodate them, they could get the market only by driving a hundred thousand other farmers out of it; who, being forced off the farm, would with their families gravitate to the city.

Farmers could be made independent of the market and so kept on the farm only in one of two ways: viz., by being so ignorant and animal that they would be satisfied simply with food and shelter, content like savages to forego the comforts of civilized life; or, by being trained to produce for themselves, in the home, the comforts which intelligence demands.

Of course the first alternative is impracticable in this land and in this day. Ignorance and stagnation can solve no problems in a republic. And the second is as impossible as reversing the

The Twentieth Century City

motion of the earth on its axis and rolling ourselves back into the age of homespun. The man capable of building for himself a comfortable house, and of making his own furniture and tools; and the woman who can learn to transform wool and flax into garments and house-furnishings, are quite too intelligent, ingenious, and competent to spend their lives thus in the midst of modern civilization. They could make a better and easier living by devoting themselves to one of their several trades, which would inevitably take them to the city.

Another conclusion to which we are forced is that all attempts to retard the movement of population from country to city by raising the standard of agriculture will prove worse than futile. It is said that if agriculture were made profitable, as it might be by scientific methods, farmers would not wish to abandon it.

A Nation of Cities

Scientific farming succeeds, because a given amount of effort, when more intelligently directed, produces greater results. Inasmuch, then, as the amount of food which the world can consume is limited, the more intelligent or scientific the farming is, the smaller will be the number of farmers required to produce the needed supply, and the larger will be the number driven from country to city. It has already been observed that if scientific methods were universally adopted in the United States, doubtless, one-half of those now engaged in agriculture could produce the present crops, which would compel the other half to abandon the farm.

We may not, therefore, take refuge in unscientific methods. If our agriculture is not improved, we shall endanger our European markets, which were worth to us in 1896 no less than $570,000,000, and gave employment

The Twentieth Century City

to 1,700,000 farm-laborers. We have been able to gain and retain these markets, notwithstanding our wasteful and unscientific methods, because of free farms of virgin soil. About 2,500,000 farms, of eighty acres each, have been given away by the Government during the past thirty years. This advantage, together with our improved agricultural implements, enabled us to compete so successfully with the farmers of Europe as to produce a general depression of agriculture there, and so to alarm the governments of Europe as to enlist their efforts in behalf of home agriculture. Ministries of Agriculture now exist in almost all countries, through which subsidies have been granted, prizes offered, agricultural academies and colleges founded, and free-lecture courses established. The people are being instructed and encouraged, and organized into co-operative agricultural so-

A Nation of Cities

cieties, which are rapidly multiplying on the Continent. Some 6,500 such societies have been formed in France, and 7,200 in Prussia; and we are told that every parish in Denmark now has its co-operative dairy.

This wide-spread revival of agriculture in Europe will force us out of their markets unless we cheapen our produce by more scientific methods, which will of course reduce the number of American farmers. If our agriculture refuses to progress, and we thereby lose our foreign markets, the 1,700,000 men now employed in producing our agricultural exports will be forced off the farm. In either case, whether American farmers accept or reject scientific methods, large numbers will be driven to the cities.

We must face the inevitable. The new civilization is certain to be urban; and the problem of the twentieth century will be the city. Many English

The Twentieth Century City

sovereigns attempted to arrest the growth of London by proclamation. Equally idle will be all attempts to turn back from the modern city the tide of population flowing up to it. One who thinks to circumvent or to successfully resist economic and social laws is fighting against the stars in their courses.

III

The Materialistic City a Menace to Itself

IT has been shown that materialism is pre-eminently the peril of American civilization, and that the city is destined to dominate the nation. Is materialism to dominate the city?

A city is not necessarily materialistic because it is rich and magnificent. The city of the Apocalypse, which came down out of heaven, and prefigures a perfect civilization—the Kingdom of God fully come in the earth—is represented as glorious beyond Oriental dreams of magnificence, and rich beyond even American dreams of wealth, but it is not materialistic. A city is materialistic in the sense intended when its intellectual and mor-

The Twentieth Century City

al development is not commensurate with its physical growth. Look, first, at the demand which the twentieth century city will make on a higher intelligence.

The development of mechanical power, which created modern civilization, took place chiefly in the city. It is not strange, therefore, that wealth has increased much more rapidly in the city than in the country. In 1850, 55.6 per cent. of our wealth was rural, and 44.4 per cent. urban. In 1890, 75.4 per cent. was urban, and only 24.6 per cent. rural. During these forty years rural wealth increased fourfold, while urban wealth multiplied sixteenfold.

Wealth, of course, is power, and the rapid increase and concentration of it creates many and difficult problems, particularly in a democracy whose institutions were framed with special reference to preventing the

The City a Menace to Itself

concentration or long retention of power. These problems, therefore, are at the same time most urgent and most perplexing in the city, where wealth is being massed; and it is there that the highest order of intelligence is needed for their solution.

The closer relations of the new civilization are emphasized in the city, and the more populations are massed, the more difficult and the more important it is to maintain good sanitary conditions. The city has been called "the grave of the physique of our race." As a rule, the denser the population the higher the death-rate. The average number of deaths for the rural districts of the United States is 14.99 in a year out of every 1,000 persons, while the average for our cities is 23.58. If we may assume that proper sanitation would reduce the average for the city to that of the country, there were, in 1890, in our cities 156,638 unnecessary deaths—victims sacrificed because we have not learned how to live in cities.

It has been demonstrated that scientific sanitation greatly reduces the death-rate. In Bradford, England, the death-rate was in twenty years reduced, by sanitary reform, from 27 to 17. In Birmingham, the average for ten years, ending in 1874, was 26.8; in 1892 it had been reduced to 20. For three years the average rate in a portion of the city was 53; sanitary reform reduced it to 21. Before the reform in Glasgow, the death-rate was 40; it is now 23.

The results of intelligent and conscientious care of the public health are shown by comparing the record of Tammany Hall with that of the recent reform administration in New York. For the ten years from 1886 to 1895, the average death-rate under

The City a Menace to Itself

Tammany misrule was 25.18. Assuming that it would have remained at 25, had Tammany continued in power, sanitary reform, by gradually reducing the death-rate to about 20 in 1897, saved 3,758 lives in 1895; 7,736 in 1896, and 9,920 in 1897—a total of 21,414 lives in three years. And, as there are twenty-eight cases of sickness in New York which are not fatal, to every one that is, we may fairly infer that sanitary reform in three years prevented 599,000 cases of sickness. Unless the tiger is more likely to change its stripes than the leopard its spots, the Tammany tiger, had it been free to ravage the city during the past three years, would, on the average, have killed nineteen victims and have wounded five hundred and thirty-nine, every day. This is but a single item of the cost of permitting unscrupulous ignorance to rule our city. The cost in money is enormous, but with that the public has generally been made acquainted.

The problems of government increase with population. As cities become more populous, relations whose harmony must be preserved increase in number and complexity. A mistake is farther reaching; it has a longer leverage; and as good government grows more essential it becomes increasingly difficult. To administer the affairs of a village of 1,000 inhabitants is a simple matter, requiring only ordinary intelligence; the government of a city of 100,000 is much more complicated; while that of a city of 1,000,000 or of 5,000,000 demands expert knowledge, ability, and character of the very highest order.

Our political development in the United States has been along national and state lines rather than municipal. The principles of the state and national governments are well settled

The City a Menace to Itself

and clearly defined, but those of municipal organization and government are confused and uncertain. We are as yet in the experimental stage, and need the insight and genius of the highest statesmanship to solve the new and complex problems of the city, which are the problems of the new civilization. Among them are those created by the industrial revolution which has taken place during the nineteenth century—such as adjusting an aristocratic system of industry to a democratic system of government.

If upon these and other municipal problems we could bring to bear the wisdom of the fathers who framed the constitution, not a scrap of it would be wasted. It does not seem to me extravagant to say that higher intellectual qualities are required to solve these problems than to administer successfully the office of the nation's chief executive.

The Twentieth Century City

Does anyone imagine that we are meeting these high demands? As our cities grow larger are we calling to office larger-minded men, capable of grappling with these profound problems? As a general rule, the larger our cities the worse and more incompetent is their government. We are permitting the most ignorant classes to control them; and, if the intelligence of a city is not brought to bear upon public affairs, it practically does not exist.

Here is an illustration of the grade of intelligence which held office in New York for many years, and which, by folly that is beyond characterization, has now been returned to power. Applicants for appointments on the police force under Commissioner Roosevelt were subjected to civil-service examination. In answer to the question, Name five of the six New England States? one man replied: "England,

The City a Menace to Itself

Oirland, Scotland, Whales, and Cork." Asked to tell what they knew about Abraham Lincoln, about twenty said he was President of the Southern Confederacy. About forty thought he was a great general in the Union army. One was sure he was "a great general who won the battle of Bunker Hill." Many thought he was assassinated by Guiteau; one said the deed was done by Garfield; and another by Ballington Booth! This would be very funny if it was not very serious.

Turn now to the increasing demands made upon moral character by the new civilization, as exemplified in the modern city.

The organization of industry, which came with mechanical power, involved the division of labor, which has substituted for the independence of the age of homespun an ever-increasing dependence.

The Twentieth Century City

Says Mrs. Browning:

> " 'Twill employ
> Seven men, they say, to make a perfect pin;
> Who makes the head, content to miss the point;
> Who makes the point, agreed to leave the joint.
> And if a man should say, 'I want a pin,
> And I must make it straightway, head and point,'
> His wisdom is not worth the pin he wants.
> Seven men to a pin, and not a man too much!"

We are told that it now takes sixty-four men to make a shoe; and each one of the sixty-four is dependent on the other sixty-three for the finished product. In like manner and measure are the great allied industries become dependent on each other. Consider how far-reaching would be the results of absolutely stopping the output of coal. All transportation by railway and steam-ship would cease. All factories dependent on steam-power would have to shut down; and those using water-power would soon be compelled to follow, for lack of trans-

The City a Menace to Itself

portation facilities. For the same reason, agriculture would be prostrated. Street-cars, whatever the power used, would come to a stand-still. Illuminating-gas, electricity, and water-supply in our large cities would all fail. Industry of every kind would be paralyzed; and, before civilization could readjust itself, famine and pestilence would sweep through the land.

Thus, as civilization grows more complex, and the individual becomes more fractional and dependent, it becomes increasingly important that men should be dependable. A moral failure on the part of a farmer, living out on a prairie, would make little difference to the world; but a moral failure on the part of a bank-cashier might prostrate the business of a community and throw thousands out of employment. Increased responsibilities imply greater opportunities for mischief, stronger temptations, and the need of

The Twentieth Century City

firmer principles. More complicated relations require a clearer perception of the rights of others, a more delicate conscience, and a keener sense of justice, for any failure of character or conduct under such conditions is farther reaching and more disastrous in its results.

It is in the city that our relations are closest and most complicated; it is there that the maladjustments of society create the sorest friction; it is in the city, therefore, that the well-developed social conscience is most needed. It is chiefly in the city that the enormous powers of organization and of centralized wealth are wielded; and it is there that these powers must feel the wholesome restraint of righteous laws and of an enlightened popular conscience. It is in the city that the unprecedented increase of wealth affords unprecedented opportunities for self-gratification; and, without a corre-

The City a Menace to Itself

sponding increase of self-control, we shall become enervated and demoralized in the lap of luxury. As the city grows populous and rich, the administration of its vast interests affords increasing opportunities for the corrupt use of money. There is, therefore, an increasing need of officials whose moral character is absolutely incorruptible—those who accept office for the public good, not those who seek it for private gain.

If, now, the citizens fail to elect such men to office, it is because the citizens themselves lack civic intelligence and civic morality. If we have not sufficient moral sense or common sense to prevent saloon-keepers, thieves, gamblers, jail-birds, and prize-fighters from dominating our municipal politics, we have as good officials as we deserve.

The character of the men who usually get control of our largest cities,

The Twentieth Century City

such as New York, Philadelphia, and Chicago, together with the corruption which has been laid open in recent years, indicates that the moral development of the city has by no means kept pace with its material growth.

It is not Chicago's moral development which has made it one of the wonders of the modern world. The president of the School Board of that city recently said in a public address: "The entire police force of this city is next to defeat in its efforts to suppress conspicuous lawlessness or to definitely arrest the career of crime within its jurisdiction." We read of a dozen highway robberies on the streets of that city in a single night. Is the moral tone of the city altogether misrepresented by the character of "the biggest man in Chicago," who is thus sketched by *The Times-Herald* of that city? "He is abso-

The City a Menace to Itself

lute master of a majority of the council. . . . As leader of the boodlers, he can suppress any measure submitted by a decent member and make it impossible for an honest alderman to put through a single piece of constructive legislation. As chairman of the finance committee, he holds the Department of Public Works, the Department of Health, the Police Department, and the School Board by the throat. He can even threaten the mayor himself. . . . Yet he is as ignorant and coarse a ruffian as would be encountered in a year's study of the slums of America. He is a saloon-keeper and gambler, the captain and associate of criminals, whose morals are beneath contempt or pity, whose daily life it is almost a shame to mention. And this is the man who holds the purse-strings of Chicago, and is permitted to dictate to public officials who, in the ordinary

The Twentieth Century City

affairs of life, would no more associate with him than with a leper." *The Times-Herald* adds: "Is there not manhood enough in public life, or power enough in the courts, or virtue in the criminal code to give this odious creature his deserts?" It would seem not.

Such abuses, resulting from a low condition of public morals, are not confined to a few of our cities. In the largest, they are most flagrant; as Mr. James Bryce says ("American Commonwealth," Vol. I., p. 608): "They are 'gross as a mountain, open, palpable.' But there is not a city with a population exceeding 200,000 where the poison-germs have not sprung into a vigorous life; and in some of the smaller ones, down to 70,000, it needs no microscope to note the results of their growth."

No moral failure is more significant in a democracy than a spirit of

The City a Menace to Itself

lawlessness, which, there is reason to fear, is on the increase in the United States. An odious law may be successfully enforced among a lawless people under a monarchy; but if in a democracy the people do not respect their own laws, what becomes of government?

Disregard of the rights of person and of property, or, in a word, lawlessness, is much more hurtful and dangerous in the city than in the country; and yet it is much more prevalent there than elsewhere. Philadelphia and Pittsburg are exceptionally good cities, but in Philadelphia there are seven and a half times as much crime to a given population, and in Pittsburg and Allegheny City nearly nine times as much, as in the average rural county of Pennsylvania.

It would seem to be sufficiently clear that the moral development of the American city has not kept pace

The Twentieth Century City

with the material; and, generally speaking, the larger the city the greater the disproportion. An inadequate intellectual growth is serious enough, but moral failure is much more so. It was the latter which proved fatal to the great civilizations of the past. Greece had no lack of intellect; hers was a moral failure. The same is true also of Rome.

What, then, is the prospect for the future? The fact that an ever-increasing proportion of population must live in the city is not reassuring as to moral growth. The decay of Italian agriculture and the migration of population to Rome accompanied and stimulated the decay of Roman morals. Mr. Lecky says: "It would be difficult to overrate the influence of agriculture in forming temperate and virtuous habits among the people." It will be much more difficult to maintain a high moral standard in a nation

The City a Menace to Itself

of cities than it would be among an agricultural people.

We have seen that the material growth of the city is to continue. The two great roots of its moral life are the home and the church. Are they as vigorous in the city as the forces which are ministering to its physical life?

We learn from the census of 1890 that of every hundred families on the farm sixty-six own their home. In cities of 100,000 population and less, about thirty-six per cent. own their homes; in cities of more than 100,000, less than twenty-three per cent.; in Boston, eighteen per cent., and in New York, six per cent. Of course, the institution of the home, with all its saving influences, may exist in the tenement, but it is less likely to do so; and it certainly cannot exist where there are several families in a single room. It is shown in Mr.

The Twentieth Century City

Charles Booth's great work, "Life and Labor of the People in London," that in that city there are 2,257,000 people who, singly or in companies, live in one room—sleeping, cooking, eating, bathing, if at all, within the same four walls. As cities grow more populous, land-values and rents increase, and the people are packed away in closer quarters. Under such conditions, hotel, lodging-house, and tenement-house populations increase, and homes decrease.

Homes are disappearing in the city at each of the two social extremes. Among the rich, hotel and club life is being substituted for home-life. With the great increase of interest-bearing securities there is a growing idle class which is migratory. They spend a few weeks in one climate and then flit to another. They have so many houses that they have no home; and their mode of life is, perhaps, as try-

The City a Menace to Itself

ing to moral character as that of the slums.

The church, like the home, grows relatively weaker as the city grows larger. In 1840 there was in Boston one Protestant church to every 1,228 souls; in 1890, one to every 2,581. In New York, in 1840, there was one Protestant church to every 1,992 souls; in 1890, one to every 4,361. Investigations show that our larger cities, generally, in 1890 had only half as many Protestant churches to the population as they had fifty years before.

Here are well-defined tendencies; growing cities, requiring for their safety an ever-strengthening moral life, while the two great moral sources of that life are steadily becoming weaker. It requires neither a prophet nor the son of a prophet to foresee the issue, if present tendencies are not arrested. James Freeman Clarke said: "A time comes in the downfall and

The Twentieth Century City

corruption of communities, when good men struggle ineffectually against the tendencies of ruin. Hannibal could not save Carthage; Marcus Antoninus could not save the Roman Empire; Demosthenes could not save Greece, and Jesus Christ himself could not save Jerusalem from decay and destruction."

The nineteenth century city is materialistic; that is, in its growth, the intellectual and moral have not kept pace with the physical. The twentieth century city can be saved from the final doom of materialism only by quickening its moral and intellectual life; for the slums, which contain the elements of triumphant anarchy, are born of the ignorance and sin of a materialistic civilization.

Speaking of an East End parish in London, where he had lived some years, Professor Huxley said: "Over that parish Dante's inscription, 'Leave

The City a Menace to Itself

hope behind, all those who enter here,' might have been written. . . . There was nothing to remind the people of anything in the whole universe, beyond their miserable toil, rewarded by slow starvation. In my experience of all kinds of savagery all over the world, I found nothing worse, nothing more degraded, nothing more helpless, nothing so intolerably dull and miserable, as the life I had left behind me in the East End of London. Nothing would please me more than to contribute to the bettering of that state of things, *which, unless wise and benevolent men take it in hand, will tend to become worse and worse, and to create something worse than savagery — a great Serbonian bog, which in the long run will swallow up the surface-crust of civilization."*

The London of to-day is a prophecy of more than one twentieth century city in the United States.

The Twentieth Century City

Saltpetre, sulphur, and charcoal are each one non-explosive, but brought together they make gunpowder. Neither ignorance nor vice is revolutionary when quite comfortable, nor is wretchedness, when controlled by intelligence and conscience. But ignorance, vice, and wretchedness, *combined*, constitute social dynamite, of which the city slum is a magazine, awaiting only a casual spark to burst into terrific destruction.

Europeans are learning, some have already learned, to live in cities. We shall find our lesson much more difficult. Their cities are singularly homogeneous and native; ours are as singularly heterogeneous and foreign. London is supposed to be cosmopolitan, and yet, in 1880, all foreign countries put together furnished only 1.6 per cent. of its population. In 1890, 49.93 per cent. of the voters of New York City, and 50.62 per cent. of

The City a Menace to Itself

those of Chicago, were foreign born, while many, in addition, were foreign by parentage. Nearly one-third of the population of our fifty largest cities is foreign by birth ; and in all of our larger cities from fifty to sixty different countries are represented.

Absolutism, as in the case of the Czar, can successfully rule a hundred different peoples, estranged from each other by race, language, custom, and religion ; but in a democracy there are many common interests which require mutual understanding and united action. The isolation, therefore, of unknown tongues, and the estrangement of race prejudice and of religious antipathy, present peculiar difficulties in American cities.

Notwithstanding all these barriers, we must reach our foreign population (and native as well), clothed with the high prerogatives of citizenship but

The Twentieth Century City

ignorant of its duties, with influences which will inform the mind and enlighten the conscience, or the twentieth century city will become a menace to itself.

IV

The Materialistic City a Menace to State and Nation

SOME sixty years ago Alexis De Tocqueville showed that the principle of local self-government is fundamental to our political institutions and to the very spirit of liberty itself. He then wrote ("Democracy in America," p. 42): "Local assemblies of citizens constitute the strength of free nations. Municipal institutions are to liberty what primary schools are to science; they bring it within the people's reach, they teach men how to use and how to enjoy it. A nation may establish a system of free government, but without the spirit of municipal institutions it cannot have the spirit of liberty."

At that time the people of the Unit-

The Twentieth Century City

ed States enjoyed local self-government, but since then important and significant changes have taken place, not wholly unforeseen by this student of American democracy. He says further: "I look upon the size of certain American cities, and especially upon the nature of their population, as a real danger which threatens the security of the democratic republics of the New World;" that is, the several states of the Union. When this was written, our urban population was less than nine per cent. of the whole; in 1890, it was upward of twenty-nine per cent., or more than three times as large, relatively.

The American city is becoming a menace to state and nation because, as it grows more powerful it is becoming less capable of self-government. The maladministration of municipal affairs in our large cities has long since become a national scandal, and

The City a Menace to the Nation

the opening up of its rottenness has made municipal democracy a stench in the nostrils of the civilized world. Our friendly but discriminating English critic, Professor Bryce, says that the one conspicuous failure of American institutions is the government of our great cities; and every intelligent man knows this to be true. Professor Franklin H. Giddings, of Columbia University, said a few months since, in an address before the Nineteenth Century Club: "We are witnessing to-day, beyond question, the decay—perhaps not permanent, but at any rate the decay—of republican institutions. No man in his right mind can deny it."

Not everyone is aware to what extent fundamental principles have been abandoned. Our Revolutionary sires thought it worth while to go to war rather than submit to taxation without representation; and as to local self-government, they deemed it the very essence of liberty. What would they have said if they could have foreseen that their grandchildren would, I will not say pusillanimously surrender these precious principles without a struggle, but actually *thrust* them out of their hands?

Our theory is that of government by the people. The municipal council represented the people, and in it was municipal government formerly centred, including, of course, the levying of taxes for municipal expenditure. But as business men became absorbed in private concerns, to the neglect of public interests, and the voters who voted failed in civic intelligence and conscientiousness, incompetent and venal aldermen were elected, and intolerable abuses naturally followed. A large majority of the voters who placed demagogues in control were non-taxpayers and regardless of the burdens laid on prop-

The City a Menace to the Nation

erty-owners. The latter class, instead of arousing themselves to their civic duties and undertaking the education of public opinion and of the popular conscience, resorted to the easier course of appealing to the state legislature, which afforded them protection from their own representatives by restricting the powers of the municipal council. These powers were transferred to independent boards, which were in no way accountable to the people. Thus our cities, for the most part, lost their autonomy and came to be governed by the state legislature, most of whose members could have little knowledge of local conditions, and would not be held responsible by their own constituents for the mismanagement of municipal affairs, in which the rural districts had but little interest.

The next step was to place the appointment of these boards in the hands

The Twentieth Century City

of the mayor, that he might be held responsible. Thus, in our larger cities power has been transferred from the legislative to the executive branch, and so centralized.

The struggle for liberty has been a struggle to wrest power from one, or the few, and to lodge it with the many; that is, to decentralize government. When popular government fails, society is saved from anarchy by the strong man; that is, power is again centralized. The movement, therefore, to centralize government by transferring power from the council to the mayor was a confession that popular government in our great cities had failed.

It has been supposed that it would be safe for the legislature to confer extraordinary powers on the mayor, because in that event the election of a man of ability and integrity would be of such transcendent importance

The City a Menace to the Nation

that the intelligence and character of the city would certainly unite to insure a wise choice.

Surely that experiment could not be tried under the stress of more powerful motives than those brought to bear in the first municipal election of Greater New York. Its mayor (or rather his boss) has in his gift offices whose salaries amount to $500,000 a year. This new government will administer municipal property to the value of $1,000,000,000, and control the annual expenditure of some $75,000,000. What an opportunity to construct a political machine! And into what master-hands has the opportunity fallen! The citizens who desired good government were in a large majority; nothing was needed to insure success, except patriotism and common sense; but they are precisely what was lacking. Under the circumstances, the failure to prevent

The Twentieth Century City

Tammany's return to power was nothing less than criminal; it was a crime against the civilization of the new century, and against the nation, because it gave encouragement to the corrupt and dangerous elements of every city in the land; and it shows that the Greater New York is as incapable of self-government as was the lesser city.

The most discouraging fact is not that so many were ignorant or corrupt enough to vote the Tammany ticket, but that the best elements in the city had not sufficient civic conscience or intelligence to sink all minor considerations and unite to defeat an organization which is known to be the embodiment of all that is foulest and most dangerous in modern municipal politics. If the light which is in a city be darkness, how great is that darkness!

It requires a much larger force to

The City a Menace to the Nation

capture a fort than to defend it. It will be much more difficult to oust the corruptionists than it would have been to keep them out. In all of our greatest cities the corrupt element is intrenched, and in successful control of methods which an English journal calls "the craftiest combination of schemes to defeat the will of democracy ever devised in the world."

Evidently democracy in our larger cities has failed. So general has become the distrust of our cities, that for years we have relied on the country vote to save the state and nation from the consequences of the city vote. And though our great cities have shown themselves incapable of self-government, they have not brought upon either the country or themselves the full natural consequences of their ignorance and corruption, because in important particulars the state has controlled and restrained them.

The Twentieth Century City

We are now prepared to weigh the gravity of the fact that more than one-half of our population will soon be urban, and that in due time we shall be a nation of cities. If the rate of the movement of population from country to city, between 1880 and 1890, continues until 1920, there will then be in the United States 10,000,-000 more people in our cities than outside of them. If the rate of growth above referred to is not sustained, it will make a difference of a few years only, as the preponderance of our city population in the near future must be regarded as certain. The cities will then no longer accept limitations from the state, but, when they have become fully conscious of their power, will take into their hands not only their own affairs, but also those of the state and of the nation.

What if the cities are then incapable of self-government? If their gov-

The City a Menace to the Nation

ernment is then "a conspicuous failure," what will become of our free institutions?

Someone will quote Lord Macaulay's saying that the remedy for the evils of liberty is more liberty; but whether this prescription is wise, or otherwise, depends. No form of government is absolutely best. That is best which secures the best results. What would be the best form for one people, would be the worst for another. Democracy is the best form for those only who have sufficient intelligence and moral character to be capable of self-government. Without such qualifications for its enjoyment, liberty lapses into license and ends in anarchy.

Judging from the record which our larger cities have made, they could not safely be intrusted by the state with autonomy; for with their present lack of civic intelligence and of civic mo-

The Twentieth Century City

rality, they are incapable of self-government.

Most of our great cities have at some time been in the hands of a mob. In the summer of 1892, within a few days of each other, New York, Pennsylvania, and Tennessee ordered out their militia, and Idaho called on the United States Government for troops to suppress labor-riots. More recent instances are fresh in mind. That is not self-government, but government by military force. There is peril when the Goddess of Liberty is compelled to lean on the point of a bayonet for support. Sooner or later it will pierce her hand.

The city, in a position to dictate to state and nation, and yet incapable of self-government, is like Nero on the throne. As the city, by virtue of its preponderating population, is soon to ascend the throne, it is well to glance at some of the powers which are reaching after the city's sceptre.

As the saloon sustains important relations to the law, it desires to control both those who make the laws and those whose duty it is to enforce them. It has already become a political institution of power. Politicians are careful not to antagonize it. Its political support or opposition is apt to be decisive; for saloon-keepers are liquor-men first, and democrats or republicans afterward. When this their craft, therefore, by which they have their wealth, is in danger, it is easy for them to drop political differences, and by uniting hold the balance of power and wield it in the interest of their business. An astute politician in New York, reputed to be a total abstainer and a church-member, said he would rather have the support of the saloons than that of the churches.

There is a Western city of exceptional intelligence, the seat of a state university—not a large city, but precisely such as we should expect to be governed by an enlightened public opinion. An ex-mayor stated in public that the city was controlled not by the people but by its one hundred saloon-keepers. "They determine," said he, "who shall be nominated and who shall be elected in both political parties."

The saloon is much stronger in the city than in the country; indeed, there are few cities in the United States which the liquor power is not able to dominate. What if the saloon controls the city when the city controls state and nation!

There is another institution grasping after political power, which, like the saloon, has its stronghold in the city. A solidified body of voters, who for any cause are not amenable to reason, and to whose individual judgment, therefore, it is useless to appeal, whether the cords which bind them into one bundle are those of appetite or of ecclesiastical authority, is dangerous in a republic.

The growing spirit of charity which thinketh no evil is slow to recognize the fact that most Roman Catholics are Catholics first and citizens afterward. The fact remains, however, and makes it possible to throw the Roman Catholic Church into a single political scale. Those who do not believe that the priesthood has both the power and the disposition to cast a substantially solid Catholic vote, simply do not know what some others do know.

It is not at all strange that those who yield the right of private judgment and accept dictation in matters of religion, should also yield the right of private judgment and accept dictation in matters of politics, especially

The Twentieth Century City

in view of the fact that Leo XIII., in his Encyclical of January 10, 1890, declared that "*politics . . . are inseparably bound up with the laws of morality and religious duties*" (*The Pilot*, Boston, February 15, 1890). This declaration, which is *ex-cathedra* and therefore binding on every good Roman Catholic, puts an end to all question whether the Roman Catholic Church claims the right to control in politics. This control is not only claimed but actually exercised, which fact accounts for the solid battalions of Tammany Hall.

This ecclesiastical power which is grasping after political control is proportionately much stronger in the city than in the whole country. In 1890 the number of Evangelical communicants in the churches of the United States was 13,869,483, while the number of Roman Catholic communicants was 6,259,265. The same census

The City a Menace to the Nation

showed, in New York, Chicago, Philadelphia, and Brooklyn, the four largest cities in the Union, 1,012,968 Roman Catholic communicants, and of all other religious bodies, Jews and Protestants, only 576,930. That is, in the whole country Protestants are more than twice as strong as Roman Catholics, while in these four largest cities, taken together, they are but little more than half as strong. The strength of Romanism is in the city, and the city is soon to dominate the nation.

Again, another fact which must be faced is that our foreign population is largely concentrated in the city.

We do not forget our indebtedness to the immigrants. They have borne the brunt of the toil and hardship in subduing the continent and in developing its resources. They shared the sacrifice to save the Union. They have enriched the literature of every

The Twentieth Century City

profession, and many are among our best citizens, intelligently and enthusiastically devoted to American institutions. But we cannot shut our eyes to the fact that the foreign population, as a whole, is depressing our average intelligence and morality in the direction of the dead-line of ignorance and vice.

About one-quarter of our foreign population is unable to speak English. There are children, born in the United States and educated in parochial schools, who are unable to speak the language of the country. A boy who had lived all his life in New York City, where he was born, was placed awhile ago on the witness-stand, and had to have an interpreter! There are some millions of foreigners among us who not only cannot speak English, but who are unable to read or write their own language. Illiteracy among the foreign-born population is thirty-

The City a Menace to the Nation

eight per cent. greater than among the native-born whites.

The census of 1890 shows that those who are foreign by birth or parentage, though constituting only one-third of the population, furnish nearly three-fifths of all the paupers supported in almshouses. That is, the tendency to pauperism among us is nearly three times as strong in the foreign element as in the native.

Again, the 20,000,000 of our population, who are foreign by birth or parentage, furnish for our penal institutions of all sorts, except juvenile reformatories, a half more prisoners than the 34,000,000 of our native white population. In other words, the tendency to crime in the United States is more than two and one-half times as strong among those who are foreign by birth or parentage, as among the native whites.

Juvenal complained that Syrian

The Twentieth Century City

Orontes had flowed into the Tiber, and brought with it its language and morals. In like manner, our American waters have been fouled by many an Orontes of the Old World.

When we consider that the quality of immigration is growing distinctly poorer, it is not reassuring to reflect that Europe could send us an unceasing stream of 2,000,000 every year —as many as our entire population in about thirty-six or seven years— and yet leave the present source of supply not only unimpaired but even increased; and until economic conditions have been equalized between Europe and America the stream will continue to flow.

Judging the future by the past, it is improbable that any legislation will dam this stream. As long ago as 1838, startling disclosures were made in regard to the immigration of imbeciles, vagrants, and criminals. Since

The City a Menace to the Nation

then, repeated action has been taken by Congress, but without substantial result. Our urban population will continue to swell by this foreign flood.

In 1890, of the male population in our eighteen largest cities, 1,028,122 were native born of native parentage, 1,386,776 were foreign born, and 1,450,733 were native born of foreign parentage; that is, those who were foreign by birth or parentage numbered 2,837,509, or more than two and a half times as many as the native American stock.

These elements, as they come to us, are clay in the hands of the political potter. If they remain uninstructed as to good citizenship, and incapable of forming individual judgments concerning public questions, the boss will certainly rule the city when the city rules the nation.

Wendell Phillips once said: "The

The Twentieth Century City

time will come when our cities will strain our institutions as slavery never did." That day is drawing near with the new century: and our probation of about twenty years is none too long in which to meet the peril of the materialistic city by building it up in intelligence and morals.

V

Remedies—The New Patriotism

In the four preceding chapters we have seen that the greatest peril to modern civilization is its materialism, that the city will dominate the future, and that the materialism of the city makes it a menace to itself, to the state, and to the nation.

These new conditions call for a new patriotism.

We all delight to honor the men who fought the battles of our country and who risked limb and life in its defence. Many of them nobly proved, what Horace sang, that

"It is sweet to die for one's country;"

but, without depreciating in the least

degree this exalted sentiment, I submit that what our country needs today is not men who are willing to die for it, but men who are willing to live for it.

There are many who in times of obvious crisis, when the bugle summons to battle, cheerfully make great sacrifices, even unto death; but who in the "weak, piping time of peace" are unwilling to give a little time and a little effort for the public good. They are too busy to attend to politics. They sacrifice the public good to private gain, which is precisely the indictment we bring against the demagogue. The men who wash their hands of public concerns are as truly responsible for municipal misrule as are the men who are in politics "for revenue only." The former neglect politics for their private interests; the latter manipulate politics for their private interests. Touching municipal affairs, they are

The New Patriotism

alike selfish; and it is the selfishness of the former which gives the selfishness of the latter its opportunity. Evidently the so-called "good citizen" is the accomplice of the bad. We are afflicted with the bad citizenship of good men. We expect bad men to be bad citizens; but when good men are bad citizens, public interests "go to the bad" with a rush.

Probably there is not a city in the United States where those who would prefer good government are not in a large majority; and yet they allow themselves to be ruled and plundered by a corrupt minority. In Europe men of high rank and of great learning deem it an honor to administer the affairs of their city; while we intrust authority to ignorant and selfish men, who give us the worst municipal government in Christendom, at four or five times the cost of good government in England.

The Twentieth Century City

Years ago, when Kossuth visited America, he said: "If shipwreck should ever befall your country, the rock upon which it will split will be your devotion to your private interests at the expense of your duty to the state." For more than a generation since then our course has been laid directly toward that rock; and in the preceding chapter it was shown that we are now within measurable distance of it.

These so-called "good citizens," who are so mindful of their own business, are not unmindful of national politics; they are probably quite concerned for the welfare of the Union, and deem themselves duly patriotic. They observe Decoration Day and hang out the flag on the Fourth of July, but are singularly indifferent as to the administration of their own city government. They are lacking in civic patriotism.

The New Patriotism

We need to remind ourselves that our political structure is based on two foundation-principles: namely, that of local self-government, and that of federation or union, which are alike necessary to the permanence of our institutions. Local self-government is necessary to the exercise of our liberties, and federation is necessary to their preservation. These two principles are like the two abutments of the Brooklyn Bridge: destroy either one, and you destroy the structure.

The principle of federation was endangered a generation ago, when we waged a great war, at unspeakable cost of blood and treasure, to save the Union. But while patriotism was at the front defending one of these principles, the other was being quietly subverted at home. Men who never had a patriotic heart-throb in their lives sought the control of our cities, not for the public good, but for pri-

The Twentieth Century City

vate gain. Circumstances favored their designs. Many immigrants had acquired the rights of citizenship who had not been instructed in its duties. It is not to be wondered at that their votes could be bought and sold in blocks of many thousands. This constituted a paradise for the demagogue, and enabled the political boss to perfect his machine and to compact his power; so that for years we have had in our larger cities, and in many of the smaller, not the government of the people, by the people, and for the people, but the government of the people by the boss and for the machine.

Our institutions are as much in danger to-day as they were a generation ago, when the principle of federation was in question. That question was long since settled, and South as well as North agrees to the integrity of that principle. But the other fundamental principle is placed in jeopardy

The New Patriotism

by our boss-ridden cities. Local self-government is to-day hanging in what Edmund Burke called "a dancing and a hesitating balance."

As
"New occasions teach new duties,"
this new peril demands a new patriotism—not new in spirit, but in manifestation ; one which is civil rather than military ; one which devotes itself to the principle actually endangered; not a patriotism which constructs fortifications and builds navies, but one which purifies politics and substitutes statesmen for demagogues; not one which "rallies round the flag," so much as one which rallies round the ballot-box ; not one which charges into the deadly breach, but one which smashes the "machine"; not one which offers itself to die for the country, but one that is willing to live for it, which is as much more heroic as it is more difficult.

The Twentieth Century City

Such patriotism calls for courage no less than that which devotes itself to military service. It calls for men brave enough to face the hatred of pothouse politicians, who are as mean as they are unscrupulous; it calls for men who dare be unpopular, who dare to be misunderstood and misrepresented; men who dare to be ridiculed and lied about and abused; men who dare to suffer in their business, and, if need be, in their bodies; men who can wait for vindication because they are working, not for applause, but for principle.

This new patriotism must be open-eyed and tireless. To keep office when they are in, and to seek office when they are out, is the business of the men who are in politics for what they can make out of it; they have nothing else to do. The people with whom is the defence of our liberties have everything else to do. When,

The New Patriotism

therefore, good citizens lose sight of the public welfare for only a little time, the rogues slip in again. The patriotism of the good citizen must be as sleepless as the selfishness of the boss and his henchmen. Eternal vigilance is still the price of liberty.

A New York brewer said: "The church people can drive us when they try, and we know it. Our hope is in working after they grow tired, and continuing to work three hundred and sixty-five days in the year." Who does not exclaim, with Dr. Parkhurst: "Oh, what a world this would soon be if the perseverance of the saints were made of as enduring stuff as the perseverance of the sinners!"

The new patriotism is stronger than partisanship. It recognizes party as only a means to good government as an end, and sees that the sacrifice of public interest for the sake of party is obvious inversion and perversion.

The Twentieth Century City

To the partisan, party success is the supreme thing, and he is willing, if need be, to sacrifice principle to it. The true patriot cares supremely for principle, and, if need be, he is willing to sacrifice party to it. The political boss differs from both the patriot and the partisan in that he cares for neither principle nor party, and is ready to sacrifice both to himself. The partisan is narrow; the boss is corrupt.

We despise the bosses, and they are no doubt worthy of all the contempt they receive, but they do not create the political situation; they are its product. When a boss disappears, whether into a prison-cell and a striped suit—where so many of them belong—or whether he retires with all the plunder he wants, or is overthrown by a stronger rival, in any case he is succeeded by another boss, who, to the methods of his predecessors, very likely adds some original villainy of his

The New Patriotism

own. The supply will be inexhaustible so long as public opinion remains uneducated and the public conscience is lethargic.

If the individual citizen is not made intelligent touching the government of the city ; if he is incapable of forming an independent and intelligent judgment, or if he fails to appreciate his responsibility as a citizen ; if he neglects the franchise, or sells it, or uses it for personal instead of public ends, there will not be lacking selfish and designing men to command an unthinking or unscrupulous following, and so control the city for private gain instead of the public good.

If the citizens generally exercised independent, intelligent, and conscientious judgment concerning public affairs, the political boss would find himself without an occupation.

This consummation, so devoutly

The Twentieth Century City

to be wished, can be reached only through patient education. We dare not rely on campaigns of enthusiasm. If tidal-waves come, they also go. If our liberties are to be secure, patriotism must be not a mere impulse, but a fixed principle, rooted in the heart, informing the mind and inspiring the life.

Such a patriotism will make this "The Heroic Age," which Richard Watson Gilder nobly sings:

" He speaks not well who doth his time deplore,
Naming it new and little and obscure,
Ignoble and unfit for lofty deeds.
All times were modern in the time of them,
And this no more than others. Do thy part
Here in the living day, as did the great
Who made old days immortal! So shall men,
Gazing back to this far-looming hour,
Say: ' Then the time when men were truly men:
Though wars grew less, their spirits met the test
Of new conditions; conquering civic wrong;
Saving the state anew by virtuous lives;
Guarding the country's honor as their own,
And their own as their country's and their sons';
Defying leaguèd fraud with single truth;
Not fearing loss; and daring to be pure.

The New Patriotism

When error through the land raged like a pest,
They calmed the madness caught from mind to
    mind
By wisdom drawn from eld, and counsel sane ;
And as the martyrs of the ancient world
Gave Death for man, so nobly gave they Life :
Those the great days, and that the heroic age.' "

VI

Remedies—Twentieth Century Christianity

JOHN ROBINSON told the Pilgrim Fathers that more light would yet break forth from the Word of God. This prophecy might be safely made in every age, because that Word reveals Him who is the light of the world, the light of every century.

The new civilization, with its new social problems, has led us to search for the social teachings of Jesus, which had been long neglected; and we find that those teachings fit modern conditions as a key fits its lock.

During all these Christian centuries this light has been beating upon blind eyes, seeking to fill them with day.

Twentieth Century Christianity

Now that new social conditions have opened our eyes to new needs, we see the light; and the prophecy of the Pilgrims' pastor is fulfilled in our own generation.

It is proposed to show in this chapter how beautifully the social teachings of Christianity are calculated to solve the social problems of the new century.

Modern social conditions have been produced by modern industrial conditions. As industry becomes more highly organized and the division of labor more complete, the interdependence of men becomes more entire, and the oneness of the life of society grows more real and more obvious. Society is beginning to arrive at self-consciousness ; that is, it is beginning to recognize itself as an organism whose life is one and whose interests are one.

With the dawn of social self-consciousness there are appearing a social

The Twentieth Century City

conscience, a new social spirit, and a new social ideal. Let us glance at each.

Conscience has more to say of duties than of rights, but the world has for centuries been familiar with the "*rights* of conscience," while the *duties* of conscience has a new, strange sound. The individualistic age, now closing, was one of self-assertion; hence, with the increasing self-consciousness of the individual came great reforms, characterized by the perception and assertion of rights. In the social age, upon which we are now entering, as social self-consciousness becomes more distinct, the awakening social conscience will perceive more and more social obligations; hence, there will be another long list of noble reforms which will demand the recognition and acceptance of duties. The watchword of the old era was "Rights"; that of the new will

Twentieth Century Christianity

be "Duties." The spirit of the old was, "I am as good as you;" that of the new will be, "You are as good as I."

This leads us to the new social spirit. We are beginning to see that the material well-being and the moral and physical health of different classes are strangely bound up in one bundle. Neither individuals, nor classes, nor nations can remain indifferent to one another. Increasing common interests are creating more of mutual sympathy. The spirit of competition is still dominant and fierce, but the spirit of coöperation is growing. The new social spirit is fraternal, and if it is not yet widely prevalent, men are at least beginning to see that the new civilization profoundly needs it.

The new social ideal springs from new possibilities. When muscles did the world's work one man could little more than provide the necessaries of life for those dependent on him. The

The Twentieth Century City

working-power of the world could be increased only slowly; and to double the number of muscles meant to double the number of mouths. Under such conditions the world could never be rich; a few might be, and were, but generally at the expense of the many. Mechanical power, on the other hand, can be indefinitely increased without any increase of population. With its advent, therefore, came the possibility of general comfort and the ultimate possibility of universal wealth.

This possibility has awakened hope, and men begin to believe that no class has been doomed to perpetual want and ignorance. Suffering is no longer deemed necessary, but rather abnormal, and social reformers feel bound to find and remove its causes. Thus, with the growth of the philanthropic spirit, the progress of science, the increase of intelligence, and the creation of wealth,

Twentieth Century Christianity

men have transferred the golden age of the world from the past to the future, and the common man has begun to dream of a perfected civilization in the far future, which has been seen in prophetic vision and sung by poets in every age.

But this new social ideal is little more than a millennium of creature comfort. It needs to be elevated, illuminated, and glorified by Christ's social ideal. It is quite possible for society to be at the same time well housed, well fed, well clothed, well educated, and *well rotted.* The world can never be saved from misery until it is saved from sin, and never ought to be. The ideal of Christianity is that of a society in which God's will is done as perfectly as it is in heaven; one in which absolute obedience is rendered to every law of our being, physical, mental, spiritual, social; and this is nothing more nor less than the

The Twentieth Century City

kingdom of God fully come in the earth. The new social ideal, dim and imperfect, when fully focussed, is seen to be the kingdom of heaven for which our Lord taught us daily to pray, and which he bade us first to seek.

In like manner Christianity meets the conscious need of a new social spirit. So far as the spirit of fraternity grows out of common interests and mutual dependence, it is only mildly unselfish and largely passive. When the social spirit has been Christianized we shall have, not a fraternity of convenience but a genuine brotherhood of love sprung from a common fatherhood. Such a social spirit will be a vital and active principle, powerful to hasten the blessed consummation of peace on earth.

Again, the awakening social conscience needs to be educated, and the teachings of Jesus contain precisely

Twentieth Century Christianity

the fundamental principles necessary for its instruction. The multiplied and complex relations of the new civilization have greatly increased and complicated our social obligations. Men are raising new questions of duty, which can be answered only by Christian ethics.

This new social conscience, this new social spirit, and this new social ideal all belong to the great social organism which is now becoming conscious of itself as a result of the new civilization. This organism is as yet extremely imperfect; how can it be perfected and the new social ideal realized?

There are two laws, fundamental to every living organism, which must be perfectly obeyed before society can be perfected; one is the law of service, the other that of sacrifice.

Every organism possesses different organs, having different functions, each of which exists, not for itself but to serve all the others. The eye sees for hand and foot and brain; the hand toils for the whole body; the brain thinks for every member; the heart beats for every fibre of the organism. If any organ refuses to perform its proper function, there is disease, perhaps death.

Again, every organism is composed of numberless living cells, each of which, we are told, possesses the power of sensation, of nutrition, of locomotion, and of reproduction. These cells freely give their lives for the good of the organism. Work, play, thought, feeling, all cost the sacrifice of living cells. If these cells were capable of selfishness, and should adopt the motto, "Every cell for itself," it would mean the dissolution of the organism. When living cells which disregard the laws of the organism enter it, and there multiply, there results typhoid fever, small-pox, diph-

Twentieth Century Christianity

theria, or some other zymotic disease. If these intruders become numerous enough to overcome the law-abiding cells of the body, the result is anarchy, which is death. Individuals may be said to constitute the cells of the social organism, and, in addition to the powers which belong to the cells described above, they are endowed with self-consciousness and will. They are therefore capable of introducing selfishness and disorder into the social organism. The great social laws of service and of sacrifice are, accordingly, very imperfectly obeyed; hence the many diseases which afflict society, and which can be cured only by bringing all men under these two laws. But how can this be done? How can selfish men be made unselfish? How can a whirlpool be transformed into a fountain?

Let us turn for an answer to the teachings of Jesus. They contain three social laws which are fundamental to Christianity ; they are the three great laws of the kingdom of God—laws which were reiterated in the Master's teachings, and exemplified in his life and death. These laws when announced seemed nothing less than absurd to the world, so utterly counter did they run to the convictions and habits of men.

The first is the law of service: " Whosoever will be chief among you, let him be your servant." In the Roman world slavery degraded labor; to serve was menial, and yet the Master took a towel, girded himself and washed the feet of his disciples. This he did for an example that they might do as he had done. " The servant is not greater than his lord." He declared that he had come, " Not to be ministered unto but to minister ;" and " As the Father sent me into the world, so send I you."

Twentieth Century Christianity

The law of service was made binding on everyone who would become his disciple.

No less binding is the second great law, that of sacrifice. He came "to give his life a ransom for many;" and he not only accepted the cross himself, but made its acceptance the condition of discipleship. "If any man will come after me, let him deny himself, and take up his cross and follow me"—follow him to the place of crucifixion whither he bore his cross. We talk of our "crosses"; he spoke of *the cross*. The word meant then what the gallows means to-day, namely, *death*. The law of sacrifice, even to dying unto self, is laid upon all who would follow Christ.

The third great law—that of love—is the most fundamental of all. It is this which vitalizes the other two. To him who loves, service is its own reward, and sacrifice is privilege. Love

The Twentieth Century City

is the fulfilling of all law, and is the root from which service and sacrifice spring. Love can transform the heart from a maelstrom into a fountain, whose rivers shall make glad the desert of life.

Two of these laws, as we have seen, are fundamental to every organism; and the third, the law of love, must become the law of the social organism before the laws of service and of sacrifice can be energized and made regnant. Selfishness is disintegrative and anti-social. Love is the antidote for selfishness; and as love is the most fundamental law of Christianity, the Christianity of Christ is, and is to be, the great social or organizing power in this new era. Thus it appears that the religion of Jesus is profoundly social, and as perfectly adapted to the saving of society as if that were its only object.

It is not strange that in an individ-

Twentieth Century Christianity

ualistic age the interpretation of Christianity should have been individualistic and narrow. The new needs of a new civilization open our eyes to the opulence of Christ's teachings and the sufficiency of Christianity for every age.

The teachings of Jesus contain the fundamental principles necessary both for the individual and for society. Exclusively they are neither individualistic nor social; inclusively they are both.

Twentieth century Christianity will instruct the social conscience, will teach that the kingdom of God fully come in the earth is the true social ideal; that the brotherhood of the kingdom creates the true social spirit, and that the three fundamental laws of the kingdom—those of service, sacrifice, and love—are the only laws by obedience to which society can be perfected.

The Twentieth Century City

In a word, twentieth century Christianity will be the Christianity of Christ, and will teach that he is the only Saviour of society as well as the only Saviour of the individual.

VII

Remedies—Twentieth Century Churches

A JAPANESE, speaking of his own country, said a dozen years ago that nothing remained as it had been thirty years before "except the natural scenery." Changes throughout Christendom, and especially in the United States, during the nineteenth century have been only less radical than in Japan. We have developed a new civilization, created, as we have seen, by the substitution of mechanical power for muscular energy, which marked the beginning of a new stadium in the march of mankind.

The old civilization was simple, the new is complex ; that was individualistic, this is collective; that was the age of homespun, this is the age of the factory; in that men were independent, in this they are dependent. Industrially, the typical family was then a little world, now the world is rapidly becoming a great family.

It was said some years ago that Christianity had done all it could ever do for mankind; that as an individualistic religion it had accomplished much for an individualistic civilization, but as civilization was now becoming collective, Christianity would of course be outgrown.

In the preceding chapter, however, it was shown that Christianity is a profoundly social religion, and as perfectly adapted to saving society as to saving the individual. What is needed, then, is the application of Christianity to the solution of the new social problems. Christianity unapplied is like power unapplied, like water

Twentieth Century Churches

above a mill-dam that is never turned to the wheel, like coal in a mine that is never raised and fired; practically, it does not exist. If this application, then, should be made, who should make it, if not the churches? This constitutes for the churches the great opportunity of the centuries. Says Dr. Charles H. Payne: "The greatest forward movement of all the ages is upon us. That movement is the saving of society, and that work the church of Christ must undertake." Not to undertake it is to break step with the march of civilization and to fall out of the ranks. If the church refuses to save society, she will fail to save herself, because she will fail to adapt herself to changed conditions. During the Christian era she has already made several important re-adjustments; and if she is to continue to live, she must make another.

The geologic record shows that at

The Twentieth Century City

times great and sudden changes took place in the fauna and flora of certain quarters of the earth. Prevalent forms of animal and vegetable life became rare or extinct, while other forms, previously rare, quickly multiplied, and filled the sea or swarmed upon the land. These wide-spread results were the effects of radical changes of climate—temperature, moisture, and the like—or of other essential modifications of the conditions of life. Those plants and animals which could not adapt themselves to these changed conditions soon perished, while others, which were better adapted, or more adaptable, throve and became dominant.

There must always be a certain measure of correspondence between all life and its environment. If the latter changes materially, the former must adapt itself to changed conditions, or die—a lesson which, in this

Twentieth Century Churches

transitional period, vitally concerns the churches. Those churches which do not accept their social mission will fail to adapt themselves to the new social atmosphere and, like extinct fauna and flora, become fossilized. Many have already perished for lack of this power of adaptation, others are to-day in a dying condition, while many more lack efficiency for the same reason.

It is the present needs of the world by which the churches must measure present duty. As Bishop Potter has said: "At such a time, for the church of God to sit still and be content with theories of its duty outlawed by time, and long ago demonstrated to be grotesquely inadequate to the demands of a living situation, this is to deserve the scorn of men and the curse of God." The churches, instead of being content with a hemisphere of truth, must teach the full-orbed Christianity of

Christ. They will be disloyal to him if they keep back his message to the new civilization.

We have seen that with the self-conscious social life of the new civilization there is being developed a social conscience. It will be one of the sacred duties of twentieth century churches to educate this conscience by applying to it the social teachings of Jesus. Surely it is one of the most obvious functions of the church to educate the conscience. It was an old and pernicious fallacy which cut life in two, dividing it between the sacred and the secular, and excluding the church from the latter. We are now beginning to see the sacredness of the secular, to understand that the sphere of religion is as broad as that of conscience, and that the sphere of conscience is as broad as life. It is no less our duty to love our neighbor as ourselves, than to love God with all our heart. Duty to our fellow-men is as binding as duty to God; indeed, duty to man *is* duty to God. We cannot be right toward God if we are wrong toward our fellows.

Religion does not consist in opinions and ceremonies, but in character and life; and we cannot live without living among our fellow-men and sustaining relations to them. These human relations constitute one-half of the sphere of the religion of Jesus; and the church which fails to instruct concerning them, and to urge the acceptance of all manward obligations, represents a very partial, not to say corrupted, form of Christianity.

The churches must both instruct and exhort concerning all duties. The new civilization has multiplied our social relations, and therefore our social obligations, manyfold. It is idle for the churches to bid us discharge our social obligations conscientiously, unless they instruct the conscience touching those obligations. Exhortation without instruction is blind leadership of a blind following; the ditch awaits both. There is no salvation, individual or social, without both a knowledge of duty and the acceptance of it. Hence the churches must both enlighten the mind and persuade the will.

If a man is living in ignorance of his duties to his fellow-men, whether those duties spring out of his social, industrial, or political relations, or, if knowing such duties he neglects them, it is as much the mission of the church to instruct and persuade him as if he were ignorant or careless of his duties to God. A Christian has duties to his neighborhood, his town or city, his state, his country, and the world; and to neglect these duties, is to sin against God. It is, therefore, the evident duty of the churches to instruct the social conscience. Pertinent to this duty, Bishop Huntington asks: "Would the church pulpit be seriously damaged or weakened in the spiritual purpose for which it was built, if abstractions, metaphysics, ritual niceties, the fine arts, literary news, ethical generalities, and well-worn exhortations were to some extent exchanged for judicious and plain instructions in Christian citizenship, and for a good-tempered application of the words and example of our Lord to society, to the uses and abuses of the power of property, and to the wrongs and cruelties which sorely obstruct the advent of the Son of Man and his kingdom?"

Again, we have seen that there is being developed a new social spirit.

As long as men differ in natural endowments, some will be more effective than others. As long, therefore, as there is selfish competition in the world

The Twentieth Century City

some will be worsted. Substitute for selfishness the spirit of universal brotherhood, and different physical and mental endowments would only increase the perfection and happiness of society, precisely as they enhance the delights of a home in which love reigns.

Love is the fundamental law of normal social life. As long, then, as that law is disregarded there must needs be social disease and soreness and distress. All attempts to regenerate society while it remains selfish must necessarily fail. Legislation, a different system of taxation, the reorganization of society, a new political party, the reformation of the old parties—all these are urged as remedies. But these, at best, are only palliative, not remedial. It is well, by every means to make it easy to do right and hard to do wrong, but the only radical remedy for our social ills is a new social spirit, the spirit of brotherhood, the spirit of love, vital enough to enter into, and to control, all relationships. This is Christ's remedy, embodied in the second fundamental law.

The churches have occupied themselves almost exclusively with the first great law, and have sought to bring men into right relations with God. They have not taken the second great law seriously, have not perceived that it is the organic law of a normal society They have not believed it to be really practicable in this selfish, sinning world. They have aimed at individual salvation; they have neglected social salvation. Indeed, they have looked upon the latter as Utopian and foolish—possible when the millennium comes, but not before. They have not believed in the practicability of the teachings of our Lord, have not believed that the Golden Rule could be lived.

The Twentieth Century City

Instances might be given, within the writer's personal knowledge, of the Golden Rule painted in large letters on the office-walls and made the working-rule of the business; of workmen sending a committee to their employer and asking that their wages might be cut down sufficiently to increase his profits to a given figure; of capitalists whose great object would seem to be, not to accumulate money but to increase the intelligence, morality, and physical well-being of their employees. The businesses referred to are eminently prosperous, and are not troubled with strikes and lockouts.

The return to Christ which is now taking place justifies the confident expectation that the existing scepticism of the churches will be overcome, that twentieth century churches will not presume to sit in judgment on their Master, pronouncing some of his requirements "practicable" and others

Twentieth Century Churches

"impracticable," but will really accept him as Lord, will really believe in him as Saviour, not only of the individual but also of society, and will dare to teach his saving truth in its blessed fulness.

Again, we may expect that the social ideal of Jesus, by reason of the return to him, will be accepted and taught by twentieth century churches as the true social ideal, for the realization of which all Christians are bound to labor.

Christ's social ideal is clearly set before us in the prayer: "Thy kingdom come, Thy will be done in earth as it is in heaven." The last clause interprets the first: the kingdom will be fully come when God's will is perfectly done in earth; that is, when all of his laws are perfectly obeyed. This includes both individual and social salvation. The two are mutually dependent. Society as a whole cannot

The Twentieth Century City

be saved unless its individual members are saved; and individuals cannot be wholly saved unless their relationships are rectified.

The full coming of the kingdom implies the abolition of all earthly ills, because every ill springs from a vicious, careless, or ignorant violation of God's laws. The kingdom fully come means the individual perfectly obedient to all the laws of his being—spirit, soul, and body—and society perfectly obedient to all the laws of the social organism; it means heaven on earth, the consummation of the

> ". . . one far-off, divine event,
> To which the whole creation moves."

The acceptance of Christ's ideal carries with it the acceptance of the social mission of the church. For what does the church exist except to realize the ideal of her Lord? The church is the body of which the head

Twentieth Century Churches

is Christ; and for what does the body exist except to do the will of the head?

The churches have generally looked upon duty as limited by the circle described around the individual as a centre. There is reason to believe that twentieth century churches will look upon duty as represented by the ellipse described around the individual and society as the two foci. The following resolution adopted by the Presbytery of New York illustrates the larger conception of their mission which the churches are gaining: "*Resolved*, That we recognize the gospel of Christ as the supreme remedy for every form of evil, and the church of Christ as the agency by which the world is to be regenerated and saved, and, therefore, we believe that the moral teachings of Christ must be applied to every sphere of life, and that the church should bear her testimony for righteousness and purity in all human affairs."

The churches are beginning to see that the gospel which Christ preached and which he sent forth his disciples to preach was "the gospel of the kingdom;" not a gospel for disembodied spirits, but one for men in the flesh; not a gospel for a fraction of the man, but for the whole man; not a gospel for isolated individuals, but one for men in an organized society—a *kingdom* coming in the earth.

They are beginning to see that their mission to the individual is no more sacred than their mission to society; and they will at length see that they have no more right to delegate society-saving, than they have to delegate soul-saving, to other organizations. Neither to society nor to the individual can the duty of the churches be done vicariously.

It has been objected that the diver-

Twentieth Century Churches

sified activities involved in the social mission of the churches would divert them from spiritual work. If this were true, the objection would be of great weight, because spiritual results must always be of supreme importance. But this objection is conclusively answered by the experience of so-called Institutional churches. These churches accept this larger view of their mission; and notwithstanding they are generally located in downtown districts, in which churches that have failed to change their methods have died, or from which they have run away to save their lives, these churches show exceptional spiritual results. Taking a denomination in which there are perhaps more Institutional churches than in any other, an examination shows that last year the Institutional churches received, on the average, more than four times as many additions on confession of faith as the average church of the denomination.

Trinity Congregational Church, Cleveland, which is three years old, reports 390 members. Lincoln Park Baptist Church, Cincinnati, is located in the midst of the "masses" which the churches find it so difficult to reach with the old methods. Out of a large membership only six families own their homes. In nine years this church has received 742 members, 562 by baptism. The Metropolitan Temple, New York (Methodist Episcopal), when its present pastor entered on his work three years ago, had 250 members; now it has 1,008. The Baptist Temple, Philadelphia, has, perhaps, the most wonderful story of any church in the world. Its work, like that of the preceding, is characterized by exceptional spiritual results. All of these churches accept the larger view of their mission, and have found

Twentieth Century Churches

it quite safe to follow the example of the Master.

Twentieth century churches, which accept our Lord's social ideal, will recognize the important distinction, which many now fail to perceive, between the church and the kingdom, and will therefore see that the church is not an end to itself, but a means to the kingdom as an end.

How often are churches located, not with reference to serving the community but with reference to the community's serving them? How often are the efforts of pastor and people directed to saving the church; seeking men in order to build up the church instead of seeking to make the church build up men? A church which exists for itself is evidently selfish, and, therefore, belies Christ. How can such a church teach the fundamental Christian laws of service, sacrifice, and love?

The Twentieth Century City

When the churches see, as twentieth century churches doubtless will, that they exist, not for themselves but for the kingdom, that like their Master they are to minister, not to be ministered unto, their services will not be "held," but rendered. What we call the services of the church are not services at all, but worship, which if genuine is pleasing to God and helpful to us. The only way to serve God that the writer knows of, is to help him do what he is doing, viz., help him lift this poor sinning, blundering, and suffering world out of its guilt and ignorance and wretchedness, into the blessedness of obedience to his laws. The way to serve God is to serve man: "Inasmuch as ye have done it unto one of the least of these my brethren, ye have done it unto me."

It is to be feared that many churches have as little of the spirit of service as Peter had when only half-discipled. "We have forsaken all," said he, "and followed thee; what shall we *have*, therefore?" Such consecration well utters itself in the ignoble lines:

> " Whatever, Lord, we lend to Thee,
> Repaid a thousandfold will be;
> *Then* gladly will we give to Thee,
> Who givest all."

A pawnbroker with a heart chipped out of flint would cheerfully give on the same inviting terms—one dollar for the return of a thousand. To give in order to get, is not giving at all; it is only investing. That is not Christianity, but business as now conducted. Oh, when shall we get rid of this commercialism in religion? Love is not commercial; it calculates no return. It breaks the alabaster box of self-concern and pours out the precious ointment of devotion without measure and without price.

The Twentieth Century City

Christ's ideal will possess the churches so far as they are possessed by his spirit; and when they have such a burning enthusiasm for the kingdom and its coming in the earth that they will joyfully render every service and gladly make every sacrifice that love can inspire, then will they be able to apply these fundamental laws of Christianity to the social organism with saving power.

VIII

Practical Suggestions

WILL twentieth century civilization be as materialistic as that of the nineteenth?

Material progress is conditioned on the control of natural forces. There is a vast storehouse of such forces not yet made available for human use. The ordinary and familiar processes of nature involve an inconceivable expenditure of energy. Professor Tyndall says: "I have seen wild stone avalanches of the Alps which smoke and thunder down declivities with a vehemence sufficient to stun the beholder; yet to produce enough snowflakes for a child to carry has required an energy competent to lift up these

The Twentieth Century City

shattered blocks and pitch them to twice the height from which they fell." The sun's heat which falls on the surface of Manhattan Island at noon is sufficient, we are told, to drive all the steam-engines of the world. The force of atomic motion is alike irresistible and immeasurable. Our present knowledge of electricity assures us of its boundless possibilities; and nature is now whispering into the ear of science some of her secrets, which suggests the possibility of giving to material civilization, within a few years, an impetus greater even than that resulting from the application of steam.

The progress of the physical sciences is astonishing. Each new discovery prepares the way for others; and our increasing knowledge of matter is giving to us an ever-increasing control of it.

The processes by which we now derive power from coal are extremely

Practical Suggestions

wasteful; even the best steam-engines utilize only fifteen per cent. or less. If the advent of cheap gas should enable us to utilize sixty per cent. of that power instead of fifteen, it would put whip and spur to material development. With modern steam-engine civilization for the multiplicand and four for the multiplier, what a product we should have!

The stores of power would seem to be as boundless as the stores of truth, but men generally are not nearly so fond of truth as of power. Physical wants, which are common to all, are far more conscious and clamorous than our intellectual and spiritual needs. What Lord Macaulay called "the tendency in every man to ameliorate his condition" acts in the Western world as a constant and powerful stimulus to material progress. Tens of thousands are seeking the rewards of inventions which economize time, power,

The Twentieth Century City

or material. A marked improvement in the physical world is quickly popularized : witness the bicycle ; not so a new truth or a new duty. They are looked at askance and regarded with suspicion even by the teachers of truth and duty, and only slowly conquer conviction and conscience. The reward for discovering a gold-mine or for inventing a labor-saving machine or process is fame and fortune. The immediate reward for discovering a truth or duty is liable to be abuse and obloquy.

In view of all these facts there is good reason to fear that the present disproportionate material development will continue, provided things are left to take their course.

We have seen that modern civilization is materialistic ; that is, the intellectual and moral sides of civilization have not kept pace with the physical. We have seen that the city

Practical Suggestions

is to dominate the nation; that the materialistic city will be a menace to the state, to the nation, and to itself.

Evidently every possible effort should be made to develop the two sides of civilization which are weak, and especially in the city. We must use every means by which the higher may gain control of the lower. Money is power in the concrete. It affords a medium through which material wealth can be transmuted into intellectual and spiritual wealth. There is a vast amount of property now used simply for the production of more wealth which should be devoted to the production of more intelligence, of more morality, of more spiritual life and power. This end can be served in part by the better equipment of agencies already at work—educational institutions and religious enterprises, which are generally kept in a condi-

The Twentieth Century City

tion of chronic embarrassment for lack of funds.

But more than this is necessary, if we are to meet the present emergency. The extraordinary situation which confronts us, the crisis of which may be reasonably expected about 1920, demands some extraordinary provision. Some means more universal and effective than any now employed must be devised for enlightening public opinion and for quickening the popular conscience. These represent the two sides of civilization which are undeveloped, and which are all-important, because more nearly than anything else human they are all-powerful. By their permission abuses exist, and by their mandate reforms triumph. By them human slavery was hedged about with "divine right," and by them it was branded as the outlawed "sum of all villainies." Concerning all laws, customs, fashions, standards,

Practical Suggestions

habits, institutions, and public policies, these two may say: "We kill and we make alive."

True as this is in general of Western civilizations, it is pre-eminently true of our own, because our government is democratic. It is especially incumbent on us to educate public opinion and the popular conscience, for, as Washington said: "In proportion as the structure of a government gives force to public opinion, it is essential that public opinion should be enlightened."

If public opinion is educated concerning a given reform—political, social, industrial, or moral—and if the popular conscience is sufficiently awake to enforce an enlightened public opinion, the reform is accomplished straightway. This then is the generic reform—the education of public opinion and of the popular conscience.

Every reform at first divides society

The Twentieth Century City

into three classes : its friends, who are few ; its enemies, who are few, and the indifferent, who are many. If the reform ever succeeds, it must win its victory from the indifferent. But how? Announce a meeting in advocacy of the reform, and it is the interested who come ; the indifferent stay away, because they are indifferent. Publish books and papers in the same behalf, and it is the interested who buy. Again, as before, we reach the ones we did not need to reach, and fail to reach precisely the ones we did need to reach.

The pulpit cannot solve this problem, for extended investigation in hundreds of towns in different states of the Union shows that somewhat more than one-half of the population do not even profess to attend any church, Protestant or Roman Catholic.

The partisan press cannot solve the

Practical Suggestions

problem, for it is not believed to be disinterested. It influences those who already sympathize with it. In the first election of Greater New York, Tammany Hall won, with the press of the city almost solid against it.

Evidently, the indifferent can be educated and aroused only by the application of the truth; and if they do not care enough for the truth to come after it, someone must care enough for it and for them to take it to them. This, of course, means systematic, house-to-house distribution of literature; not, however, by pastors. They would need to be miraculously multiplied, like the loaves and fishes, in order to supply so great a multitude. But there is ready at the hand of almost every pastor a force quite equal to so vast a work, and waiting to be organized into the needed instrumentality. Reference is made to the various young peoples' societies, which have

The Twentieth Century City

so marvellously multiplied in recent years. The Endeavor Societies, the Epworth Leagues, the Baptist Unions, the Brotherhood of St. Andrew and that of Andrew and Philip, the Luther League, the Young Men's and Young Women's Christian Associations have an aggregate membership in the United States of more than four millions. If one in ten of these young people, all of whom are avowedly enlisted for Christian service, should distribute a dozen leaflets once a month, they would reach five million families with sixty million leaflets in a year. One-half of these families would be non-church-goers, and presumably one-half or more would be destitute of all reform literature.

Let the pastors provide for the districting of the community, including from one to two dozen families in a district, according to the number of messengers available. Even the scat-

Practical Suggestions

tered houses of country districts can be included, because easily reached by means of the bicycle. The young people will require no special training for the work and no peculiar fitness, except faithfulness and common courtesy. Let the pastors enlist them, assigning them to their respective districts, decide what line of reform should be taken up first, select the leaflets best adapted to local needs, and the young people will carry on the work without laying any burden on pastors already overburdened.

Such endeavor will do as much good to the young people as they will do to others. Many of them are already engaged in active Christian work, but many more are in danger of gaining the impression that Christian activity consists in attending meetings and taking part in them. They need to engage actively and systematically in the service of others. Such service as

The Twentieth Century City

has been suggested will soon acquaint them with the religiously destitute localities both in city and country, and naturally interest them in the establishment of Sunday-schools and other religious agencies. Thus the religious truths in which they have been instructed will be wrought into the fibre of their own Christian character while they are helping to form public opinion and to quicken the popular conscience.

Of course the value of the work will depend on the value of the literature distributed. It must be such as the people will read, and adapted to all degrees of intelligence; no goody-goody stuff, more likely to reach the waste-basket than the conscience and heart, but strong, true, bright, attractive, and thoroughly healthy.

Such leaflets are now in preparation by some of the most eminent writers, statesmen, editors, clergymen, and educators in the land, and a sufficient

Practical Suggestions

number with which to begin the work are already in hand. Their cost is only nominal, and when divided between the churches or the young people's societies, it is insignificant.

Some of these leaflets should be locally prepared and deal with local conditions. In a political campaign an important service may be rendered by first carefully verifying facts concerning the characters and records of unworthy candidates and of unfaithful officials, and then giving them wide publicity in a non-partisan way. An association of citizens in Boston so exposed an unworthy candidate for the mayoralty as to force him to leave the city. The Municipal Voters' League of Chicago, which publishes the records of all candidates for public offices, condemned twenty-eight out of thirty-four aldermen whose terms were expiring, as unfit; and only two of the twenty-eight were re-elected.

The Twentieth Century City

Such a course on the part of churches or pastors is not "going into politics." By exposing unworthy men, irrespective of party affiliations, they will help to separate municipal elections from state and national politics: which fundamental reform, by the way, should be effected at an early day; for when the cities are in a position to dictate state and national policies, it will be vastly more difficult to disentangle state and national politics from municipal elections.

In each state there should be made a digest of the liquor, Sabbath, gaming, and such other laws as relate to morals and good order; also a leaflet giving the duties of city, town, and county officials, together with their oaths of office. Knowledge of the fact that the public is well acquainted with the law will often bring officials up to duty, and such acquaintance also serves to prevent the violation of law. Fur-

Practical Suggestions

thermore, knowledge of the law serves to strengthen public opinion as to its enforcement. Such leaflets can be prepared and furnished for a fraction of a cent.

It is astonishing to what an extent the people are ignorant of their own laws and of the duties of their own public servants. If they knew as little of their private concerns, we should soon be a nation of bankrupts. This ignorance accounts largely for the lack of public spirit, and especially for the apathy in regard to the violation of many laws.

Again, foreign Americans are not made acquainted with our institutions. The need of rudimentary instruction is illustrated by the case of the Italian who, after he had taken out his first naturalization papers, was in doubt whether this country was an empire or a kingdom. A judge of Los Angeles, California, tells us that he asked a foreigner, applying for naturalization, why he desired to become an American citizen, and he naïvely replied, " So that I can sell my vote."

Let there be prepared for our foreign population a series of leaflets dealing with such subjects as the following : The Meaning and Value of Naturalization, The Rights of the Naturalized Citizen, The Duties of the Naturalized Citizen, The Value of a Vote, Fundamental American Institutions, and the like. Such leaflets, translated into as many languages as may be necessary, would be gladly received, and serve as a social pepsin to aid our national digestion, greatly facilitating the assimilation of these foreign elements into the body politic.

No one can estimate the educational value of such a work. The proposed medium for reaching the

Practical Suggestions

people would be equally available for every kind of needed literature, whether distinctly religious or moral, dealing with temperance, Sabbath, social, or political reform. It suggests possibilities fully equal to the magnitude of our needs.

And, quite apart from the advocacy of any reform, there is increasing need of a healthy, cheap literature, as an antidote to the poison which is now being brought within the reach of almost every man, woman, and child in the land. Corrupt and corrupting newspapers have become well-nigh as ubiquitous as the vermin of an Egyptian plague.

When the object in publishing a paper is to serve the public good, journalism is a profession, and the editor an educator. But when that object is simply to make money, journalism becomes a business, not a profession, and the editor a mere caterer, who aims to tickle the appetite of the public. The management deems itself bound to furnish whatever is demanded by that appetite, however morbid it may be; and as the appetite grows by what it feeds upon, the tendency is from bad to worse. The taste of hundreds of thousands has been educated down to a point where now it can feast on filth.

In addition to the sheets which make a specialty of sensation, vice, and crime, thousands of tons of fiction, cheap in every sense, circulate through the mails as second-class matter at special rates. "Blood-curdling" stories for boys and girls are a large part of this stuff. Its character may be judged from titles taken, almost at random, from thousands of the same kind: "Manhattan Mike, the Bowery Blood," "Red Skin Tom, or the Demon's Trail," "Eagle Kit, the Boy Demon," "The Girl Avenger," "The

Practical Suggestions

Girl's Dead Shot," "Wild Emma, the Girl Brigand," etc., etc. Some thirty-six million pounds of this matter are foreign novels, among which are the filthiest French publications, outlawed in England, and recently even in France, but which can legally corrupt the morals of American youth. To carry this foreign fiction alone would require annually 900 freight-cars, each loaded with 40,000 pounds of books.

But worse than all this is the obscene literature which is being circulated with devilish ingenuity and persistency for the purpose of corrupting children and youth. No decent person can imagine its character. It might have come from the cesspool of perdition. This literature circulates so secretly that very few have any conception of its extent or of the festering corruption which it works.

The possibilities of the press, both

The Twentieth Century City

for good and evil, suggest William Cowper's ode to it:

" How shall I speak thee, or thy power address,
Thou god of our idolatry, the Press?
By thee, religion, liberty, and laws
Exert their influence, and advance their cause.
By thee, worse plagues than Pharaoh's land befell,
Diffused, make earth the vestibule of hell;
Thou fountain at which drink the good and wise;
Thou ever-bubbling spring of endless lies;
Like Eden's dread probationary tree,
Knowledge of good and evil is from thee."

The good press is the only adequate means for fighting the bad press. We have made bad literature cheap and common: we must make good literature cheaper and more common. The remarkable success achieved by Mr. Harmsworth of London during the past ten years demonstrates that it is possible to drive out bad literature with good. A few years ago the iniquitous "penny dreadfuls" of England had an enormous circulation among boys. The attractive and

Practical Suggestions

healthful publications of Mr. Harmsworth have driven hundreds of them out of existence.

A general elevation of the popular taste will do more to suppress the nastiness of the scavenger press than the most Draconian law. But the elevation of the popular taste and the education of public opinion and of the popular conscience are not all. When public opinion has been enlightened and the social conscience quickened, they need to be applied to the national life. We have now no medium through which an aroused popular sentiment can be brought to bear quickly and effectively upon state and national legislation. We are liable at any session of any legislature to have bills introduced which do violence to the conscience of the state. bills which outrage the convictions of all respectable citizens have been rushed through and made laws, simply because there was no medium through which popular indignation could quickly utter itself. Again, good bills fail to become laws for a like reason, because popular pressure cannot be effectively brought to bear upon the legislature.

If liquor-men or gamblers want special favors at the hands of legislators, with large experience and large pocket-books they know precisely how to bring influence to bear. Honest citizens are preoccupied with their own business, and most of them do not know that an outrageous bill has been introduced until it is enacted into law. Those who know of the obnoxious measure and disapprove of it cannot leave their business and go to the state capital to fight it, though they would gladly sign a protest against it. Legislators accordingly yield to the pressure which is brought to bear, and gratify a small but urgent

Practical Suggestions

minority. Not long since a local-option pool bill was introduced into the Connecticut Senate by a member who said that there were two elements in all communities, and that one element had asked him to urge the adoption of the bill and the other element had not objected. He accordingly proceeded to advocate this bill, which granted local option in gambling; and, notwithstanding it would have been disapproved by four out of five of the citizens of the state, if brought to their attention, the bill was passed.

The people may disapprove a bad bill or desire some important reform measure like the passage of the Anti-Lottery Bill, which was enacted by Congress in 1895; but what is everybody's business is nobody's business. Occasionally, as in the instance just cited, a man is sufficiently heroic and public-spirited to make the common concern his own, and sacrifices time, money, and it may be health, in order to bring public opinion to bear in behalf of needed legislation. Slowly and laboriously he secures names of influential men in all parts of the country, and by personal correspondence urges them to write their Congressman or Senator. Again and again at different stages of the bill's progress he appeals for more pressure. He must prepare great quantities of literature and scatter it broadcast. He must be habitually on his knees before the public, begging for money with which to push the work. He must be at the capital, open-eyed and resourceful, to meet the unscrupulous tactics of the opposition. He must fight the devil in the shape of corrupt lobbyists and of venal law-makers; and if, after many months of toil, day and night, he is finally successful, it will be because he combines many high and exceptional qualities.

Practical Suggestions

Shall great reforms, on which untold interests hang, depend on the remote chance of arousing precisely the right man to undertake such a work?

Nine out of ten of the citizens of a state might be favorable to a given measure, without anyone's being willing to make the personal sacrifice necessary to crystallize the existing public sentiment and bring it to bear on the legislature.

But when a state has been organized and districted as suggested above, and a properly constituted board of representative and trusted men agree that a bill pending in the legislature ought to be pushed through, it will be quite practicable in four or five days to procure and place before the legislators a petition from hundreds of thousands of their constituents. Of course opposition to an obviously bad bill can be as quickly and effectively

The Twentieth Century City

brought to bear as influence in favor of a good one.

Whenever names are secured in sufficient numbers to indicate unmistakably the will of the multitude, it will amount practically to the *referendum*, and be morally certain to determine the action of the people's representatives. Speaking of the multitude, Professor Bryce says ("American Commonwealth," Vol. I., p. 455): "American legislatures are horribly afraid of it, and, indeed, of any noisy section of it. They live in the breath of its favor; they hasten to fulfil its behests almost before they are uttered."

Thus the same agency employed to educate public opinion can be utilized to focus it upon the law-making body; and as rapidly as the popular conscience is educated concerning proper subjects of legislation, its declarations can be crystallized into law.

In the twentieth century city will

Practical Suggestions

meet most of the great problems of the new civilization. We have seen that the Christianity of Christ is beautifully adapted to solving those problems, and we have seen that it is the duty of the churches to make the needed application. By the method above described they can inspire, guide, and consummate all of the reforms demanded by applied Christianity.

This work will require a measure of coöperation, but we need not wait for it until we can all subscribe to the same creed, and accept the same form of church government. John Wesley said: "Though we cannot think alike, may we not love alike?" And surely those who love alike may join hands in works of love, which without coöperation would be impracticable. Is there not in every community enough of love, patriotism, and sanctified common-sense to make such coöperation practicable and actual? And in view of the limited probation of this nation, is it not time to act NOW?

Speaking of the anti-slavery reform, Theodore Parker once said: "The trouble is I am in a hurry, and God isn't." I think he was precisely wrong. God is in a hurry, and his people are not. If there is any reason why sin and sorrow should ever cease, it is a reason why they should cease as soon as possible. If there is any reason why the Kingdom should ever come, there is the same reason why its coming should be hastened. If God were willing to have a single pang of needless woe in the world, he would not be an absolutely benevolent being. Hence, speaking after the manner of men, God is in a hurry; he is infinitely urgent; he is saying to his people: "Come ye up to the help of the Lord against the mighty."

The city is to control the nation:

Practical Suggestions

Christianity must control the city; *and it will.* The first city was built by the first murderer, and crime and vice and wretchedness have festered in it ever since. But into the last city shall enter nothing that defileth, neither shall there be any more sorrow nor crying, for the former things shall have passed away. Shelley said: "Hell is a city much like London," but the city redeemed is, in the vision of the revelator, the symbol of *heaven* — heaven on earth—the Kingdom fully come.

INDEX

	PAGE
Adaptation, necessity of, on the part of the churches	133–135
Agriculture, effect of scientific	50–53
In Europe	52, 53
Influence of, on machinery, 34–37; on morals	72
Allegheny City, crime in	71
Anti-Lottery Bill, passage of	175, 176
Antoninus, Marcus	76
Baptist Temple, Philadelphia	148
Berlin, growth of	31
Boss, the	112, 113
Boston, Protestant churches in	75
Browning, Mrs., on division of labor	64
Bryce, Mr. James	70, 83, 178
Burke, Edmund	109
Calcutta, growth of	31
Chicago, "the biggest man in"	68–70
Government of	68–70
Growth of	34
Percentage of foreign voters in	78
Christianity of the twentieth century	116–130
Churches of the twentieth century	131–152
Cities built since 1800	21
City, the Apocalyptic	55, 181
Control of, by saloon, 93, 94; by ecclesiastics	94–97
Decrease of churches in	75
Decrease of homes in	73, 74
Demands of the, on increasing intelligence	56–63
Demands of the, on increasing moral character	63–67
First and the last	181
Government of, still experimental	60, 61
Growth of, inevitable	43, 44
Growth of the modern	29–32, 33–54
Materialistic, the, a menace to itself, 55–80; a menace to state and nation	81–102
Preponderance of, in 1920	90, 91
Sanitation of	57–59
Wealth of	56
Civilization, old and new	131, 132
Clarke, James Freeman	75
Churches, duty of, to educate the conscience	136–139
Duty of, to teach Christ's second law	139–143
Duty of, to society	143–149

Index

	PAGE
Commonwealths organized during this century	21
Communicants in the United States, number of Evangelical, 96; of Roman Catholic, 96; in four leading cities	97
Conscience, a social	118
Education of	122, 123, 136
Power of the popular	158, 159
Cowper, William	172
Cross, the, and crosses	127
Death rate in city and country	57, 58
In Bradford, Birmingham, and Glasgow	58
In New York	58, 59
Democracy, failure of, in large cities	89
Democritus	17
Demosthenes	76
De Tocqueville	81
Distribution, lack of	36
Education, necessity of	114
Energy or working-power of the nation	23
Engel's law	41
England, harmonious development of	15
Europe, agricultural revival in	52, 53
As a market for our agricultural products	51, 52
Municipal government in, as compared with our own	105
Farms brought under cultivation	22
Given away by the government	52
Farming, effect of scientific	50–53
Fiction, French	171
Food, over-production of	35
Giddings, Professor Franklin H.	83
Gilder, Richard Watson	114
Gladstone's estimate of world's wealth	19, 20
Golden Rule in business	142
Greater New York, first election in	87, 88
Municipal property and expenditure	87
Greece, degeneration of	15, 16
Hannibal	76
Harmsworth, Mr.	172, 173
Homespun, age of	45
Horace	103
Huntington, Bishop	139
Huxley, Professor	76
Ideal, a new social, 119–121; Christianized	121, 122
Indifferent, reaching the	160, 161
Industry, organization of	45, 46
Intellectual progress	27–29
Immigrants	97–101
Crime among	99
Indebtedness to	97
Illiteracy of	98
Pauperism among	99
Strength in city	101

Index

	PAGE
Jesus Christ could not save Jerusalem	76
Jesus, social laws of	125-130
Social ideal of	143-146
Journalism as a profession and as a business	169, 170
Kossuth	105
Leaflets for the million	161-168
Lecky on moral influence of agriculture	72
Legislation, bringing the popular conscience to bear on	173-178
Leo XIII	96
Lincoln Park Baptist Church, Cincinnati	148
Literature, corrupt and corrupting	169-172
London, East End of	76, 77
Growth of	31, 54
Percentage of foreigners in	78
Love, law of	127, 128
Lucretius	17
Materialism of American civilization	20-25
Of modern civilization	11-32
Macaulay, Lord	91, 155
Mechanical power: its application to agriculture and manufactures produces opposite effects	38-41
Substituted for muscular, effects on growth of city	37-41
Merchandise annually transported by rail	23
Metropolitan Temple, New York	148
Moral progress	27-29
Nero	92
New York, growth of	30
Percentage of foreign voters in	78
Protestant Churches in	75
Odessa, growth of	31
Parity of growth necessary	12
Parker, Theodore	180
Parkhurst, Dr.	111
Patriotism, the new	103-115
Must be courageous	110
Must be open-eyed	110-111
Payne, Dr. Charles H.	133
Philadelphia, crime in	71
Phillips, Wendell	101
Pittsburg, crime in	71
Population, increase of our	21
Loss of, in rural districts	34
Redistribution of	34
Power, concentration of, in city	84-86
Potter, Bishop	135
Principles, two fundamental, on which our political structure is based	107
Production, increase of	46, 47
Public opinion and the popular conscience, power of	158, 159
Rail, merchandise transported by	23
Railway, effect of, on growth of city	41, 42
Railways, construction of	22
Referendum, the	178

Index

	PAGE
Reform, the generic	159
Remedies	103–181
Robinson, John	116, 117
Roman morals, decay of	72
Romanism in politics	94–97
Strength of, in city	96, 97
Rome, degeneration of ancient	15, 16
Growth of	31
Roosevelt, Commissioner, civil-service examination under	62, 63
Sacrifice, law of	124, 125, 127
Saloon, influence of, in politics	93, 94
Sciences, increasing knowledge of	16–18
Self-consciousness of society dawning	117
Service, law of	123, 124, 126
Churches that know little of	150–152
Shelley	181
Society divided into three classes by every reform	159, 160
Soil, back to the, a fallacious cry	44–50
Spain, failure of	15
Spirit, a new social, 119; Christianized	122
Steam-power of United States, Great Britain, Germany, and France	18
St. Petersburg, growth of	31
Suggestions	153–181
Tammany Hall, sanitary conditions under	59
Solid vote of, accounted for	96
Telegraph lines, miles of	23
Trinity Congregational Church, Cleveland	148
Tyndall, Professor	153
Washington	159
Wealth, effects of	25–27
Increase of national	24
Increase of world's	19, 20
Wesley, John	179
Working-power or energy of the nation	23
Young people's societies	161–163